Arms Control
and Nuclear Weapons

Recent Titles in
Contributions in Military Studies
Series Advisor: Colin Gray

Arms Control and Nuclear Weapons

U.S. POLICIES AND THE NATIONAL INTEREST

Edited by
W. Gary Nichols and Milton L. Boykin

Contributions in Military Studies, Number 59

GREENWOOD PRESS
New York • Westport, Connecticut • London

Library of Congress Cataloging-in-Publication Data

Arms control and nuclear weapons.

(Contributions in military studies , ISSN 0883-6884 ;
no. 59)
Chiefly papers originally presented at the Citadel
Symposium on Arms Control and Nuclear Weapons, sponsored
by and held at the Citadel, Charleston, S.C., 1985.
Bibliography: p.
Includes index.
1. Nuclear arms control—United States—Congresses.
2. Nuclear arms control—Soviet Union—Congresses.
3. United States—National security—Congresses.
4. United States—Military policy—Congresses.
5. Soviet Union—Military policy—Congresses.
I. Nichols, W. Gary (William Gary) II. Boykin,
Milton L. III. Citadel Symposium on Arms Control and
Nuclear Weapons (1985) IV. Citadel, the Military
College of South Carolina. V. Series.
JX1974.7.A6727 1987 327.1'74 86-29429
ISBN 0-313-25389-7 (lib. bdg. : alk. paper)

British Library Cataloguing in Publication Data is available.

Library of Congress Catalog Card Number: 86-29429
ISBN: 0-313-25389-7
ISSN: 0883-6884

First published in 1987

Greenwood Press, Inc.
88 Post Road West, Westport, Connecticut 06881

Printed in the United States of America

The paper used in this book complies with the
Permanent Paper Standard issued by the National
Information Standards Organization (Z39.48-1984).

10 9 8 7 6 5 4 3 2 1

Contents

Acknowledgments

Several individuals and organizations stimulated and
supported the preparation of this book. First and
foremost we acknowledge the generosity of The Citadel
Development Foundation, which provided funds for
individual research, conference participation, and
sponsorship of The Citadel Symposium on Arms Control
and Nuclear Weapons, 1985. We are also indebted to
Major General J. A. Grimsley (Ret.), President of The
Citadel, and to Brigadier General G. F. Meenaghan, Vice
President for Academic Affairs of The Citadel, for
their encouragement and administrative support.

Foreword

"Arms control" and "nuclear weapons" are phrases that
appear on the front page of every newspaper virtually
every day and are heard on the television news programs
almost every night. Yet the former is largely
undefined in the average citizen's mind and the latter,
even though understood, conjures up such unpleasant
images that the same average citizen chooses not to
dwell on it for any length of time. Therefore, however
often repeated, the phrases are little comprehended and
for many cause an unconscious rejection. This results
in a situation in which we have two subjects mentioned
and talked about as much as the World Series in October
and addressed substantively and conmprehendingly as the
theory of relativity at any time. This is an
unfortunate and even dangerous state of affairs;
happily, some steps are being taken to ameliorate it,
and one of them is the conference which gives rise to
this volume.

Shortly after Robert Hutchins retired as
Chancellor of the University of Chicago, he was asked
with acerbity by one of his critics if communism was
still being taught in the college; he replied in the
affirmative, noting that cancer was still being taught
in the medical school. Important subjects, indeed
matters of life and death, however unpleasant or
depressing, must be taught and discussed if we are to
understand them and deal with them objectively and
intelligently. It is therefore important for
conferences such as The Citadel Symposium on Arms
Control and Nuclear Weapons to take place and address
issues such as the military-nuclear balance,
proliferation, negotiations, and the like. Such
consideration in turn creates a basis for looking
beyond these more current problems and addressing
over-all questions of long-range policy, in particular
the question of whether deterrence, as we know it now
and have known it for over forty years, remains a
viable and defensible policy, or whether it should be
discarded in favor of what some see as a more moral and
less dangerous posture, that of defense.

This last question, which has always existed in
the nuclear era, has, of course, risen to the fore in
the minds of the public (and of the two super powers)
as a result of President Reagan's proposal in March,
1983, for a strategic defense initiative (SDI) - the
so-called "Star Wars" defensive system. Given the
enormous cost of such a system, if it is pursued, and,
even more important, in light of the absolutely crucial
impact which decisions regarding SDI can or will have
on our strategic policy, on our relations with our
allies, on our treaty-making and treaty-compliance, and
on our political as well as military posture vis-a-vis
the Soviet Union, it is imperative that our
decision-makers, and indeed the public at large, have
before them as much information and analysis as
possible. This can only be achieved by open discussion
and, as appropriate, argument, dissent and criticism.

The next war, if there is one, will be our last,
for a nuclear war between the super powers will
effectively destroy civilization as we know it. It is
therefore mandatory that every means available to us be
used to prevent such an outbreak and the use of these
weapons and their delivery systems (which,
paradoxically, represent in one sense a tribute to our
technological genius and skills while at the same time
epitomize man's willingness to expose himself to
self-annihilation). One important avenue leading to
such prevention is the process of informing ourselves
about these weapons, their history, our past efforts to
limit them and the possibilities for their future
control, limitation and reduction.

What follows is, I believe, a valuable and
significant contribution to this education imperative
and one that should achieve the widest possible
readership and given the closest possible attention.

Ralph Earle, II

Abbreviations

ABM	Anti-Ballistic Missile
ASAT	Anti-Satellite System
CABM	Conventionally Armed Ballistic Missile
COMECON	Council for Mutual Economic Assistance (Communist-bloc nations)
C3I	Command, Control, Communications, and Intelligence Capabilities
FBS	Forward-Based Systems
GLCM	Ground-Launched Cruise Missiles
ICBM	Intercontinental Ballistic Missile
INF	Intermediate Nuclear Forces
IRBM	Intermediate Range Ballistic Missile
KGB	Komitet Gosudarstvennoi Bezopasnosti (State Security Committee, USSR)
MAD	Mutual Assured Destruction
MASS	Mutually Assured Security
MIRV	Multiple Independently Targeted Reentry Vehicle
NASA	National Aeronautics and Space Administration
NATO	North Atlantic Treaty Organization
SACEUR	Supreme Allied Commander Europe
SALT	Strategic Arms Limitation Talks

SDI   Strategic Defense Initiative

SLBM   Submarine-Launched Ballistic Missile

SSBN   Nuclear-Powered Fleet Ballistic Missile
               Submarine

START   Strategic Arms Reduction Talks

Arms Control
and Nuclear Weapons

1

Introduction: The Recent History of American-Soviet Arms Control Negotiations

George M. Seignious, II

In the Carter Administration, arms control was such a centerpiece of expectations by the American people that most ended up disappointed. It is too easy for governments and for citizens to be overly optimistic about what can be obtained through measures of arms control. While increases in armaments add to distrust, they are basically caused by distrust. The closed Soviet society with its atmosphere of secrecy and its ideology of continuing struggle against all that are not a part of the socialist camp is in fundamental conflict with the Western and non-allied nations which are attached to the concepts of individual freedom, open societies, responsible government, the rule of law, and peaceful settlement of disputes. This fundamental mutual opposition, even rivalry, and the resultant distrust, are at the very core of East-West relations, and give rise to increasing danger as both sides seek to maintain and improve their military forces, both conventional and nuclear. The very measures perceived by one side as necessary for defense are all too often taken for offensive measures by the other and contribute to a higher sense of instability, a wariness, and a lack of confidence that the future can hold any safety or well-being for the human race. If one side should obtain or even pursue a perceived advantage, the other may, and usually does, either seek similar weaponry, take defensive measures, or pursue further countermeasures to negate the advantage that the other side has achieved, or is perceived to have achieved. One side could, on the other hand, impel the other to look for security through negotiations and substitute what they perceive to be an inadequacy for redress under a negotiating process. To let you understand that this isn't a new perception about the seriousness of the situation we are in, I want to quote from a speech made by a great American at St. Alban's School in Washington on November 5, 1957, almost 30 years ago.

The central problem of our time, as I view it,
is how to employ human intelligence for the
salvation of mankind. It is a problem we have put
upon ourselves, for we have defiled our intellect
by the creation of such scientific instruments of
destruction that we are now in desperate danger of
destroying ourselves. Our plight is critical, and
with each effort we have made to relieve it by
further scientific advance we have succeeded only
in aggravating our peril. If we are going to save
ourselves from the instruments of our own
intellect we had better soon get ourselves under
control and begin making the world safe for
living.

That speech was given by General Dwight
Eisenhower's principal ground commander, the man in the
Army who commanded more troops in battle than any other
American in history, General Omar Nelson Bradley, our
last five-star general. That quote from a
distinguished soldier underlines the imperative nature
of the serious business in which we are involved in
trying to find a solution and a limitation of nuclear
weapons. I want to consider briefly how we got where
we are and the meaning of our position. Remember that
during the 1950's and 1960's we in America had such a
preponderance of nuclear power compared to the Soviets
or anybody else in the world that we were able to adopt
in the Eisenhower Administration a strategy called
"Massive Retaliation," and we could base our plans as
military strategists on assertions that we were willing
to use tactical and strategic nuclear weapons against
conventional attack whenever this was militarily
advantageous.
    This is a period in history that is gone. Even in
1961, when President Kennedy came into office, we
sought to deemphasize nuclear retaliation and to create
the ability to fight limited wars and
counterinsurgencies, thus returning to a more
conventional emphasis which had prevailed in the Truman
and Acheson days. Don't forget, however, 1962. This
is the year the Soviets retreated from their placement
of missiles into Cuba. At that time they made a
commitment that never again would the United States
have the political leverage stemming form its base of
nuclear power to cause the Soviet Union to withdraw
ignominiously from a political and military endeavor.
They have seriously committed themselves to this
proposition ever since that time.
    They started developing intercontinental ballistic
missiles by the gross, and by the end of the 1960s had
developed large, although crude systems. They had
increased their inventory of intercontinental ballistic
missiles to exceed anything we had, and their
production was such that we felt that we had to

negotiate some control on that production. Thus was
born SALT I.

SALT I represented an asymmetrical condition. The
Soviets had produced more delivery systems, but we had
a qualitative advantage because we had gone to multiple
independent re-entry vehicles (MIRVS). By the time the
SALT I process was negotiated and completed in 1972,
the United States had come to accept fewer launchers
than the Soviet Union had because we had multiple
warheads that could be shot from each of our missiles.

There are two major parts of SALT I which are
important for any student to remember. One is that the
offensive systems were asymmetrical. They had more
launchers than we did, but we were comfortable with
that situation at the time because we had more warheads
that could be shot from each missile. The second
important ingredient of SALT I, which has proven to be
much more lasting, is the Anti-Ballistic Missile (ABM)
Treaty. For the first time in the history of this
country and for the first time in the history of the
Soviet Union, each super power agreed on a policy of
vulnerability. The agreement still exists today,
because that treaty is in perpetuity, whereas the
treaty on offensive systems was for five years and was
called an interim treaty. But the Anti-Ballistic
Missile Treaty recognizes that no city, no institution,
no population in the United States would be protected
from intercontinental ballistic missiles. Therefore,
and until this moment, Charleston, Washington, New
York, The Citadel, Notre Dame, Harvard, the
Metropolitan Opera, any institution we hold dear, is
subject to nuclear attack without any defense. The
same is true in Kiev, Moscow, and anywhere else in the
Soviet Union, because neither side has adequate
defenses against intercontinental ballistic missiles.
We have what is called a deterrent, that is, an
offensive nuclear capability so strong that if they
attempt to strike us they know perfectly well that we
can decimate them in very short order. And that is the
mutual deterrence policy or so-called mutually assured
destruction, that we have been operating under for
years.

SALT II was intended to redress the asymmetrical
number of launchers accepted under the SALT I Treaty.
It was supposed to not only provide for an equal number
of launchers for each side, but also to put qualitative
constraints on the most threatening aspect of nuclear
systems, the intercontinental ballistic missiles of
which the Soviets had so many more than we. We were
trying to limit the number of missiles and also to
limit the number of warheads on each. This negotiation
went on for seven years.

When the negotiations started, neither the Soviet
Union nor the United States had highly accurate
systems. The Soviet systems in particular were not
very accurate. So at no time in the early stages of
SALT II were our intercontinental ballistic missiles

overtly threatened by a complete wipe-out. In other
words, we weren't completely vulnerable. Because of
the longevity of the negotiations, however, and the
assiduous application of technology by the Soviets, by
1978 they had improved their accuracy tremendously,
enabling their ICBMs seriously to endanger our
fixed-base ICBMs.

The treaty, although not perfect, did achieve some
goals by putting ceilings on numbers, albeit very high
ones, which permitted us to build up our forces, and
forced them to reduce their forces nominally by 10
percent. Constraints were put in SALT II on the number
of warheads in their biggest missile, the SS-18. It
was limited in warheads to what had been tested, which
was 10 warheads. The United States, incidentally,
expects to have 10 warheads on its MX missile when it
is deployed. But this was a nominal step toward
codifying a limitation on strategic arms. We think we
achieved at least one step in what must be understood
as a long process.

Another achievement concerned the verifiability of
what we negotiated. Because their systems are very
large and our intelligence-gathering capabilities are
high, it was not too tough to verify the terms of that
treaty when we signed it in 1979. I believe the
Soviets are being less than honest about their
compliance with both the SALT II Treaty and the ABM
Treaty. That puts at severe risk in an open society
such as ours the whole process of arms control. If
treaties are signed and not complied with, they become
a threat to our security rather than a protection.

The SALT II Treaty, however, was not ratified
after it was signed in Vienna in June 1979. The
political judgment to force two major treaties on the
United States Senate in the course of twelve months was
a high-risk proposal. The President made the decision
that he wanted the Panama Canal Treaty ratified and
that he wanted to move immediately after that to have
SALT II ratified. There were many senators
representing fairly conservative states who did not
want to spend their political capital voting for both
of these major treaties in such a short time. Senator
Howard Baker from Tennessee was a good example. He
went out on a political limb and supported the
ratification of the Panama Canal treaty. When it came
time for SALT II, he was most hesitant to return to his
constituency and say that he was going to support
another treaty, this one involving an element of trust
in dealing with the Communists. Many other moderate
political leaders similarly backed away.

In late 1978 we had practically wrapped up our
negotiations with the Soviets when other problems
arose. Ten days before Secretary of State
Cyrus Vance and I were to meet Foreign Minister Andrei
Gromyko in Geneva, National Security Advisor Zbigniew
Brzezinski convinced President Carter to invite Chinese
Premier Deng Xiaoping to Washington in January 1979.

This was the time President Leonid Brezhnev tentatively had agreed to come to Washington to sign SALT II. When Secretary Vance and I arrived in Geneva, we found the Soviets furious at the prospect of sharing billing with the Chinese. They proceeded to throw up obstacles which delayed the signing until six months later. SALT II was now thrown into the arena of the presidential elections that started in that summer of 1979.

As the campaign heated up, Senator Frank Church, Chairman of the Senate Foreign Relations Committee and responsible in the Senate for conducting hearings on the ratification, seized upon the existence of a Soviet brigade in Cuba to try to bolster his chances for re-election in Idaho. He held up the ratification process, stating that we would not proceed until the Soviets withdrew their brigade from Cuba. His proposition was a bogus one, because that unit, a training unit, had been in Cuba for fifteen to twenty years, and had been much larger at one time. This episode is an example of domestic politics taking control of a serious treaty-ratification process. I have said since that it was also the first time in history that an Idaho potato ever derailed a strategic treaty. Unfortunately that is not all that happened.

Other moderate senators were willing to support the treaty provided the administration agreed to seek funds for long-term programs authorized under the terms of SALT II. Various battles over the budget and other issues resulted in the failure to provide a convincing five-year plan for weapons permitted by the treaty. Senators like Sam Nunn of Georgia, a dedicated and knowledgeable student of our defense, were unwilling to take the lead in support of the treaty. One important issue is the ability of our intelligence community to keep us apprised of Soviet capabilities and compliance with the treaty. Shortly after the Iranians seized in their country our two intelligence-collecting sites, called the Taxman Stations, I was testifying before the Senate when Senator John Glenn of Ohio asked me to evaluate the impact of this loss on our intelligence-gathering capabilities. Senator Baker was also present, and I said, "Let me put it this way. Senator Baker could have a hole in his cheek, a gash in his throat, and his image would not be whole, but we would all still be able to recognize him. After about nine months or a year that hole would be filled, that gash would be gone, and the image would be restored by other means." Thereupon Senator Church slammed down the gavel and said, "Let the record show that Senator Baker does not have a hole in his head." Then, of course, came the invasion of Afghanistan in December 1979. President Carter consequently withdrew the SALT II Treaty from consideration by the Senate.

The sequence of events since SALT II has seen the Reagan Administration progressively build our defenses, reversing a trend that had been adverse for fifteen years, and developing a tough negotiating stance. In

the Strategic Arms Reduction Talks (START), serious
efforts were made to reduce the Soviet force structure
that was most threatening, namely their intercontinental ballistic missiles. These efforts did not
get very far.

In addition to START negotiations, of course, was
the Intermediate Nuclear Force negotiation, conducted
by Ambassador Paul Nitze. These talks were the result
of the Soviets' setting up a missile system called the
SS-20 that could target Rome, London, and Paris,
indeed, all of the NATO alliance. It could not target,
however, the United States. This situation led Helmut
Schmidt, the Chancellor of Germany, to question whether
the United States would maintain its commitment to
defend Western Europe from Soviet nuclear attack. His
concern resulted in an allied agreement in December,
1979, called the "Dual Modernization Decision," in
which we agreed to modernize our Pershing missiles and
deploy 572 ground-launched cruise missiles. This
number would not be enough to offset what the Soviets
were doing, but would be sufficient to maintain the
U.S. nuclear commitment to the alliance. As soon as we
began the deployment of these missiles, in December
1983, the Soviets walked out of both sets of talks.

Although arms control talks have since resumed in
Geneva, negotiations between the United States and the
Soviet Union continue to be handicapped by the
asymmetrical nature of their nuclear forces. Whereas
the United States had maintained a general balance of
ICBMs, submarines, and bombers, the Soviet Union, in
contrast, has kept 75 percent of its strategic forces
in fixed-base ICBMs. As we improve the accuracy of our
systems, the Soviet strategic force becomes
increasingly vulnerable, and they become less willing
to reduce it. If we proposed and they established a
balance of strategic forces, the asymmetrical nature of
the force structure steadily would diminish. As these
forces become more symmetrical it would be somewhat
easier to negotiate mutual and equal reductions. To
ensure our ultimate goal of eliminating nuclear
weapons, we must together set even higher goals, such
as mutual survivability and a just balance of forces
for all. Only within the shared framework of these
ideals can we ever hope to find solutions to the grave
questions of arms control and nuclear weapons.

PART 1

The Future of
Arms Control

2

The Future of American-Soviet Arms Control Negotiations: The Strategic Defense Initiative Debate

Kenneth L. Adelman

I am pleased to report that 1984 is behind us. It was many things, but it was not at all the year George Orwell had depicted. Rather, it was a year in which the Soviet-type government continued its downward slide, becoming less--not more--attractive around the globe. Wars in sundry regions troubled us, but the perpetual wars of Orwell's imagination were nowhere upon us. So much the better.

Instead, 1984 was most significant in what did not happen by the 15th of May. On that day, the world broke the modern record for length of time without major war. The old record, just short of 39 years, was set between the battle of Waterloo (1815) and the outbreak of the Crimean War (1854).

The year marked another significant unfolding: the increasing discourse surrounding--and at times, even enveloping--the Strategic Defense Initiative (SDI). Over the coming years, this subject will surely dominate our discussions on arms control, deterrence, and military strategy, if indeed its domination of our subject is not evident already. Even now it is paramount in the parlors of America dealing with security issues.

PREDICTING THE FUTURE

The starting point for any rational discourse on SDI--and many discourses on SDI have not been rational, but have been wrapped in and warped by emotion--is a large dosage of modesty at predicting what science can offer in the future. How many times in our history has human ingenuity overcome human expectations and even predictions. To take just a few examples:

● Thomas Edison forecast:
Fooling around with alternating currents is just a waste of time. Nobody will use it, ever. It's too dangerous . . . Direct current is safe.

- Simon Newcomb noted in 1903:
  Aerial flight is one of that class of
  problems with which man will never be able to
  cope.

- Lee De Forest argued in 1926:
  While theoretically and technically
  television may be feasible, commercially and
  financially I consider it an impossibility, a
  development of which we need waste little
  time dreaming.

- Admiral William Leahy, Chief of Staff to
  President Truman, warned in 1945:
  The [atomic] bomb will never go off, and I
  speak as an expert in explosives.

From these examples, and many more besides, one is
humbled out of blithely accepting the word of all those
so-called "experts" who now go on and on about how a
strategic defense can never work, can never be
cost-effective, can never be stabilizing. They may
well turn out to be just as short-sighted in retrospect
as many of their predecessors have been in hindsight
today. If these "experts" turn out to be technically
correct, if the SDI research does not pan out, this
will be an unpleasant reality, but reality nonetheless.
We will have to accept this disappointing judgment--but
always with the hope that the vision can someday be
realized.
Likewise for some similar "experts" in our field
of strategic affairs. Many today are raising protests
about SDI's alleged strategic or geopolitical
shortcomings. Quite frankly, if the SDI research
proves successful, the prevailing strategic thinking
would need to be revised. This is never easy, but
almost inevitable in human endeavors. Periodically we
need to reexamine long-held assumptions and beliefs, to
question the conventional wisdom. Conventional wisdom
is not always forever wise.
Deterrence has worked. In fact, deterrence has
been a smashing susccess, as I offered in my opening
homage to May 15, 1984. For the past few decades,
however, its success has hinged upon that dreadful
"balance of terror" that came to be called Mutual
Assured Destruction. This strategy, of course, is
based on the conviction that if the United States
retains the capability to inflict unacceptable damage
in retaliation against Soviet aggression, the Soviet
Union will be deterred from embarking upon such
aggression in the first place. Long before it was
dubbed MAD, Winston Churchill captured its essence:

It may well be that we shall, by a process of supreme irony, have reached a stage in this story where safety will be the sturdy child of terror, and survival the twin brother of annihilation.

Some supreme irony, hanging over modern existence like some looming sword of Damocles. Such a condition has naturally come under question and then under attack from persons across the entire ideological spectrum--from the most liberal to the most conservative, and many of us in between. These misgivings are not, of course, just a recent phenomenon; they go back for years.

Admittedly, deterrence based on the threat of nuclear retaliation will remain the prevailing approach for the next decade or more. If we take the necessary steps to maintain the strategic balance, and if we diligently pursue nuclear arms reductions, such a posture of deterrence can continue to preserve the peace unless and until something better comes along, just as it has these nearly 40 years.

THE CHALLENGE TO NUCLEAR DETERRENCE

Why challenge this approach? Quite simply, because it is such a disturbing situation. It is disturbing to contemplate--particularly for any American President--that the ultimate response to large-scale aggression is the threat of annihilation. If possible, the President should have options, not just the one button. If another button to destroy incoming nuclear weapons might be feasible, shouldn't we look into that possibility?

On another level, there are several factors which, in my view, underscore the need we have to research the possibilities of moving towards a strategy of protection, one that places greater emphasis on defense against nuclear weapons, that moves us away from any prospect of global extinction.

First, components of defensive technology have progressed markedly over the past decade or so. Though we do not know exactly what the future holds for defensive technologies, any more than Einstein knew what the future held for nuclear energy, we do know that the research holds considerable promise. The SDI research effort is a reasonable bet. Much of it stands at the very frontier of today's scientific and technological advancements--in computers, in sensors, in radars, in high-energy particle beams, and in lasers.

Surely a good deal of the technical picture has changed since we last engaged the Soviets in a dialogue on the relationship of offensive and defensive forces. That was in the 1960s and early 1970s, on the road to the Anti-Ballistic Missile or ABM Treaty.

To take a relatively simple example: For many years now it has been assumed--and correctly so, to date--that defenses against ballistic missiles were not and are not cost-effective. No matter how much defense one side deploys, it still appears cheaper for the other side to overwhelm those defenses with decoys or even with more offensive systems.

That equation and others may change with future technologies. If so, SDI can then prove a real incentive to deep reductions in offensive nuclear systems through arms control. We hope for that kind of incentive from SDI.

At the same time, however, we must scrupulously guard against a vicious cycle of defensive efforts--even research for defense--spurring the other side onto more offensive weapons in order to saturate prospective defenses, and so on, and so on. That snowball effect would undercut stability and weaken deterrence.

The ultimate value of SDI depends, of course, on a lot more than just cost-effectiveness. The President's program is designed to answer as well:

- What technologies offer the most promise?
- How practical, how effective will systems based on those technologies prove to be?
- What countermeasures can the offense take and can they in turn be countered? At what cost?
- Can any defensive system be made survivable, recognizing that vulnerable systems would be destabilizing?
- How could such systems best be integrated into the strategic forces of each side to help stabilize the strategic relationship?

No one has a crystal ball in this complicated business. We need data to provide a sound basis for decisions several years off on whether to pursue strategic defensive systems further. If the answers to one or more of the above questions proves negative, that answer alone could tilt the decision away from proceeding further. On the other hand, if the answers to the above questions prove positive, a managed evolution--one involving the Soviets and the Allies intimately all along the way--could lead to a safer world.

To elaborate on one often-raised question--that of SDI's ultimate effectiveness--we can surmise already that even less than a so-called leak-proof defense, less than a perfect defense, could reduce the risk of war. For it could markedly increase a potential attacker's uncertainty about the likelihood of success of its attack. An that, after all, is the quintessence of deterrence.

We need not go far for examples. The survivability of our command, control, communications, and intelligence capabilities, or C3I, is critical to effective deterrence. Although it often gains little attention, strengthening these capabilities has been the first priority in President Reagan's strategic modernization program for several years. Furthermore, the growing vulnerability of our fixed land-based ICBMs has been a worrisome development since the 1970s. The purpose of the SDI research program is not focused on finding a defense for a few components, but is much broader. However, if in this process we find that survivable defenses could make our C3I or ICBM components more survivable, deterrence would be correspondingly strengthened.

Similar arguments pertain to Allied assets. In fact, contrary to what some critics are alleging, SDI will not decouple the United States from its Allies. Nor will it mean a return to "Fortress America." Americans have learned that there is no such fortress, that there can be no retreat.

A less-than-perfect defense could also hold out hope against an unauthorized or unintended nuclear attack--the kind of nightmare that was dramatized in the novel Failsafe some years back. Meanwhile, a President has no alternative but to ride out the destruction of a city or two in response to such a "mistake," or retaliate in kind. Not a desirable alternative; more of a Hobson's choice. Thus, the second factor propelling us towards greater emphasis on a defensive strategic posture--after the technical promises today's efforts may offer--is the hope it offers to reduce the risk of war by moving us away from complete vulnerability towards active protection.

A third factor for questioning current wisdom is the ethical dimension. There is some resemblance today between the debate on the morality of deterrence and the current debate on the wisdom of SDI. We deploy nuclear weapons not to use them but to make war against the United States and our Allies far less likely. In this same vein, if we find that some defensive systems can reduce the risk of war, then morality should drive us hard in that direction.

This ethical dimension is seen in the over 1,000 American clergymen who have publicly endorsed SDI research. It is also seen when one of the original proposers of the U.S. Catholic Bishops' Pastoral Letter in 1983--Bishop O'Rourke of Peoria, Illinois--strongly urges "a vigorous pursuit" of strategic defensive systems.

For the same impulse that drove the bishops to question the dreadful reality of today's nuclear predicament should--and in some cases does--drive them towards the hope of greater reliance on defensive efforts. They do not miss the point--often overlooked in other discussions--that SDI is focused on non-nuclear defenses against nuclear weapons. It is part of an effort to move the world away from nuclear weapons.

Fourth and last, but by no means least, SDI research is valuable in furnishing us greater understanding of the advanced technologies that might confront us. The Soviets have been conducting a vigorous research program for some years now. To use the jargon, SDI is a "prudent hedge" against the Soviet Union's active defensive programs and research, particularly its potential to break out of--or creep out from--the ABM Treaty.

Not only has the Soviet Union constructed its one permitted ABM site around Moscow, but other activities in conjunction with the Moscow system suggest that the Soviets may be moving toward a nationwide ABM system. President Reagan's second report to Congress on Soviet non-compliance problems, just recently issued, addresses this concern. Soviet non-compliance in several areas is a serious matter. Among other problems, it undermines the confidence essential to an effective arms control process in the future.

The Soviet Union has an extensive air defense program, besides continuing its vigorous research on lasers and on neutron particle beams for strategic defenses. In fact, overall, the Soviet Union spends some ten times more than the United States on defensive programs.

Even more startling, over the past decade and a half since the signing of the ABM Treaty, they have spent roughly as much on strategic defense as on strategic offensive forces. Maybe they understand the benefits of defense better, or maybe they don't. In any event, surely the worst outcome of all would be to tie our own hands on research on defensive systems while the Soviets go ahead and gain substantial advantage in this realm.

THE ABM TREATY AND SDI

It is useful to remind ourselves that the U.S. SDI research efforts are fully consistent with our treaty obligations, particularly under the ABM Treaty. Eventually some modifications to these obligations may be warranted to permit more definitive demonstrations or transition to a more stable balance that includes defenses. If so, these would need to be addressed mutually with the Soviet Union.

Meanwhile, we are in strict conformity. Research on defensive systems is not only permitted under the ABM Treaty but was actively advocated when we entered into that agreement. When the treaty stood before the U.S. Senate, Defense Secretary Laird noted that we would "vigorously pursue a comprehensive ABM technology program." Indeed, active research programs on ABM technology have been supported by every U.S. President since then, though not with the same interest or emphasis as President Reagan has shown.

The main threats to the ABM Treaty lie, not in SDI, but elsewhere. First and foremost, the threat lies in the Soviet Union's violation of the ABM Treaty's provision with its new radar being built as Krasnoyarsk. This Soviet construction is most disturbing. They had to know that, eventually, we would detect such a massive structure, several football fields large. Construction had to have been planned in the early-to-mid-1970s, the heyday of detente. Yet they proceeded.

Second, the ABM Treaty was founded on an assumption that limits on defensive systems would be swiftly followed by limits on offensive systems. As our SALT Negotiator, Ambassador Gerard Smith, noted at that time:

> Because of the special importance that the U.S. attaches to the relationship between defensive and offensive weapons limitations, a formal statement was made putting the USSR on notice that if an agreement providing for more complete offensive arms limitations were not achieved within 5 years, the duration of the Interim Agreement, U.S. supreme interests could be jeopardized and should that occur, it would constitute a basis for withdrawal from the Treaty.

The assumption that significant offensive limits would follow soon has not yet come true, primarily due to Soviet unwillingness to agree to deep reductions in strategic arms.

One of our major objectives in the upcoming arms control negotiations will be to reverse the erosion of the ABM Treaty that has occurred over the last decade. We will be prepared to discuss future defensive systems as well as existing systems--space-based as well as ground-based--that can attack objects in space or that use space to attack targets on earth.

BACK TO BASICS

Most broadly, we will be going "back to basics" in looking at the relationship between offensive and defensive forces. We will be describing to the Soviets, in some detail and with some care, the kind of strategic concept that will guide us in the period ahead. We envision it as falling into three phases.

During the first phase, deterrence will continue to rest almost exclusively on offensive nuclear retaliatory capabilities. We believe that this can be done at greatly reduced levels of nuclear forces and with full compliance with the ABM Treaty, and we will seek both. We hope the Soviets believe and will act likewise. This period could last ten or fifteen years, or longer or even indefinitely, depending largely on the progress and results of the ongoing SDI research.

The second phase will be one of transition.
During this period, and assuming successful development
of some effective non-nuclear defensive systems, we
would begin to move towards a strategic posture with
ever-greater reliance on defense rather than offense.
A transition of indefinite duration, this period will
help lay the technical and political groundwork
necessary for the ultimate goal of eventually
eliminating nuclear arms completely.

The last period will have as its hallmark the
complete elimination of nuclear arms. The technical
knowledge of how to make these weapons and the danger
of cheating would persist. These risks, unfortunately,
can never be eliminated, but effective defenses would
give insurance against them. The enormous and
depressing nuclear threat hanging over the world could
be lifted.

These three stages have to evolve gradually and,
as I stated, depend critically upon a cooperative
effort between the United States, in consultation with
its key allies, and the Soviet Union. Unilateral
moves, or seeking unilateral advantages, would almost
surely be destabilizing. This principle and others
were explicitly recognized in the points that emerged
during Prime Minister Thatcher's Camp David meeting
with President Reagan.

Months of extensive and painstaking top-level
analysis, ranging from questions of tactics to the
overall U.S.-Soviet strategic relationship, must
precede any arms control negotiations. A critical
ingredient in this process is the direct and heavy
involvement of the President at every step.

After the recent Shultz-Gromyko meetings I
traveled to Yugoslavia, Hungary, and Romania to provide
East European leaders with U.S. impressions of and
perspectives on the Geneva sessions and the larger arms
control picture. The most interesting single moment
occurred in Romania.

My high-level host for lunch at one of the finer
restaurants in Bucharest expounded at length on the
benefits and virtues of the Communist system.
Throughout this praise, I could not get my mind off the
fact that I could see my every breath in the cold room
and longed for more garments.

Finally, I asked my host if there were not such a
thing in Communist doctrine as objective reality. I
suggested that the facts of little warmth, little
light, and economic hardship reflected that reality and
were the true commentary on the darkness and frigidity
of the Communist system itself.

That story exemplifies the deep political and
ideological differences between East and West that
cannot be reconciled through arms control. I tell the
story, however, not to underline those differences, but
to try to keep us all in a realm of objective reality.

Despite the profound differences between East and
West, there is a shared interest in avoiding a

catastrophic military confrontation and a shared
opinion that we have to get on with the task of
reducing--and eventually eliminating--the nuclear
threat. Getting back to basics, back to the
offense-defense relationship, may be just the
prescription for overcoming the impasses in arms
control thought to date and for finally transforming
our deepest desires into a far safer future.

NOTES

1. Quoted in Norman R. Augustine, Augustine's
Laws (Washington: American Institute of Aeronautics
and Astronautics, Inc., 1982), pp. 186-89.

2. House Armed Services Committee, Full Committee
Hearings on the Military Implications of the Strategic
Arms Limitation Talks Agreement (Washington: U. S.
Government Printing Office, July, 1972), p. 15087.

3

An Analysis of the Strategic Defense Initiative (SDI)

Molly Ravenel

One of my long-held beliefs and the reason that I am an active member on the governing board of Common Cause is my conviction that the average citizen has the ability to be involved effectively in public policy questions. So often we feel that something highly technical like this--the business of arms control, the business of advances and increases in technology in weapons systems--is not understandable by an ordinary person. You have to know all your facts or you can't deal with it. I hope that you will agree with me that the subject is overwhelming only in its implications but not in the sense that it is incomprehensible. I write in this vein as a citizen, a concerned citizen, who has trust in our mutual common sense.

THE FEASIBILITY OF SDI

There are many who would argue with Ambassador Adelman about the Strategic Defense Initiative. We need to address ourselves first to the feasibility of developing this system. Then we need to consider whether such an initiative might be interpreted as another round in the arms race which could be counter-productive to serious arms talk.

To begin with, there is the problem of what might be called "seductive labelling." The claim made by the President, a little less so by others, is that SDI would possibly render nuclear weapons obsolete. For that claim to be valid, we need to remember that as long as a few weapons get through, we would have an unacceptable level of destruction.

Assuming the system is leak-proof, would it be helpful to the situation? Mr. Adelman, in his paper, suggests that it would create uncertainty for the Russians and lessen their ability to trust their offensive system; but does uncertainty really help to create stability and lead to the kind of trust that General Seignious talked about in the Introduction to this book as necessary for productive arms control talks? It is unlikely that uncertainty necessarily contributes to stability.

SDI AS A PROTECTIVE SHIELD

There are other problems in assuming that SDI is a truly protective shield which we can trust to eliminate the threat of offensive nuclear weapons. In the first place, it does not deal at all with bombers or cruise missiles. Since SDI is only concerned with ICBMs, there are several categories of nuclear interchange from which we are not shielded. Second, SDI needs to work perfectly the first time, and since it cannot be fully tested, its effectiveness is unknown. Third, it depends on satellites in space that are very vulnerable. Ballistic missiles move; most satellites remain in a fixed position relative to the earth and are highly visible. What the President and others have called Mutually Assured Security (MASS), is merely a costly escalation of Mutual Assured Destruction (MAD). Although an appealing concept, perhaps too appealing, it may highly attract people to a defensive system that is both flawed and destabilizing.

Since Hiroshima, we have seen that one advance in arms development leads to another countermeasure in what seems to be an endlessly spiraling cycle. We have to keep that historic perspective in mind. The administration is talking in terms of a major turnaround, but this view needs to be questioned. Should we be skeptical or hopeful that SDI will lead to a mutual scale-back of offensive weapons? As a destabilizing development, SDI may indeed be just another step up the escalation ladder.

The vulnerability of orbiting elements in space reduces the response time to terrifying levels. We are not talking about a 30-minute warning anymore, but a response which would require a hair trigger. We are talking about a few seconds to make a decision about the appropriate response to a military threat.

SDI MAY FACILITATE A FIRST STRIKE

Another dangerous factor is that it is possible, and in fact is argued by the Soviets, that the development of SDI looks like a move toward a first-strike capability rather than toward the defense of our population centers. This is not the United States perception, nor our stated purpose, but it is easy to see how the Soviets could think this. Here is the United States continuing with the development of offensive weapons, such as the cruise missile and the MX, and at the same time embarking on a major defensive system which would prevent an effective retaliatory strike. The end result, if both systems are effective is an unchallenged first-strike capability. The

Anti-Ballistic Missile (ABM) Treaty represents our
mutual recognition of this danger twenty years ago. We
would certainly be very uneasy if the shoe were on the
other foot and this combined development were occurring
in Russia.

It has also been suggested that SDI would prevent
nuclear accidents. Are there not other less
threatening and cheaper ways to do that? One's systems
can be manned with a command disable capacity on both
sides. This is a much cheaper way to prevent
accidents. It all sounds like Mission Impossible, but
again that is the sort of world we are talking about
here.

We must realize the threat SDI poses to the ABM
Treaty, which prohibits defense systems beyond the
laboratory stage. Since it is unlikely that Congress
would approve research and development of a weapons
system we do not plan ever to deploy, the research on
SDI implies that we might eventually violate the ABM
Treaty. In the Scowcroft Commission Report, General
Scowcroft says that "the strategic implications of
ballistic missile defense and the criticality of the
ABM treaty to further arms control agreements dictate
extreme caution in proceeding to engineer developments
in this sensitive area." (Scowcroft, et al., Second
Report of the President's Commission on Strategic
Forces.)

ASATS: ANTI-SATELLITE SYSTEMS

Another intimately related area of development is
what we call ASATs or Anti-Satellite Systems. The
Soviets have voluntarily, as I understand it, agreed to
do no further ASAT testing as long as we don't. Our
system is much more advanced than theirs, so this seems
to be to our advantage. Because ASAT development
involves testing in space, the verification problem is
less intense and therefore is an area where we should
expect progress in arms control talks. Instead of
accelerating competition in this area, perhaps we
should consider restraint.

At the moment we observe a moratorium imposed by
Congress on ASAT testing. Satellites, colloquially
called "eyes and ears of a nation," are important
information-gathering vehicles. Anti-satellite
developments which threaten those eyes and ears are
extremely destabilizing. In human terms, we are keenly
aware of how dependent we are on our eyes and ears, and
anything that would wipe them out would leave us
feeling most vulnerable. Surely this is true on the
national level as well as on the individual level. We
should continue this moratorium.

Some of our leaders have indicated that SDI is a
hedge against other Soviet breakthroughs in strategic
nuclear defense. The theory is that if we get there
first, it will discourage them from reliance on ICBMs.

This strategy could backfire. It could create more
uncertainty and simply lead to an effort to build even
more ICBMs to penetrate the shield.

    These are critical issues, and it is important to
consider seriously the alternative approaches presented
by informed people. If there were easy answers to all
the questions there would be little debate. Our first
step toward arms control should be the continuation of
the ASAT moratorium, and the second step, a halt in
nuclear testing. We had seven years of negotiations in
the last round of arms control talks and huge
technological changes came about during those seven
years. Given the pace of negotiations today, even more
destabilizing changes could take place in the course of
current arms control discussions. These two steps
would have a stabilizing effect that would promote the
essential element of trust in building the path to arms
control.

4

A Critique of American-Soviet Arms Control Negotiations

Milton L. Boykin

In the best Socratic tradition, it is wise to remember that the beginning of knowledge is the recognition of ignorance. This seems particularly true when it comes to working out adequate arms control agreements. To mention only a few difficulties, there is skepticism about the motivations and intentions of our adversaries, there is limited information about the number and disposition of Soviet weapons systems, and there is uncertainty about what the future holds in the areas of science and technology and how these developments will affect national security. There seems to be little doubt, however, that there are no sensible military uses for nuclear weapons, and there are far too many of them in the world today. The purpose of this chapter is, first, to explore some of the difficulties in working out adequate arms control agreements, and second, to stress the importance of arms control as a major tool for insuring our survival while we search for a more adequate means of protecting our national security.

Despite the many problems associated with the arms control process, a serious political commitment is essential if we are to stabilize the arms race. The Reagan Administration came into office claiming that for the last ten years arms control negotiations had been used to hoodwink the American people. Tough talk of "godless demonic forces" has receded into the background, but the depth of the United States commitment to the arms control process is questionable, although it would seem that President Reagan would genuinely like to leave the world with fewer nuclear weapons than he found it. Although the Soviet Union advocates "peaceful coexistence" and apparently sees arms control as one way to reduce the dangers of nuclear conflict, the violations of previous treaties raise doubt about the depth of their commitment.

One must be cautious in claiming too much for arms control. There is legitimate doubt concerning the efficacy of arms control even to provide a short-term solution to the problems of stabilizing the arms race.

It would be unfortunate if arms control, even if
successful, were to lock us into a permanent policy of
having to threaten the world with nuclear destruction
in order to preserve our national interest. Long-range
policy goals regarding moral alternatives to the policy
of Mutual Assured Destruction should not be forgotton
in our enthusiasm for stabilizing the current balance
of military power.

It is possible that eventually a political
accommodation can be reached which will assure the
security interests of both East and West. Even
shortrange military defense strategies are sensitive to
contemporary economic and political considerations.
The decision of Eisenhower to emphasize nuclear
deterrence in the first place was highly motivated by
economic as well as social considerations. The
continued reliance on tactical nuclear weapons in
Europe as part of the NATO strategy of "flexible
response" and "forward defense" is in part at least a
result of the unwillingness of our European allies to
increase their defense expenditures for the purpose of
building an adequate conventional military force. One
of the main arguments for the recent deployment of
Pershing II and cruise missiles in Europe was to
"couple" American and European defense interests.
European leaders feared that unless we had Intermediate
Range Nuclear Weapons in Europe to retaliate against an
attack of the Soviet SS-20s, the United States might
abandon the Europeans to their fate. If so much of our
nuclear debate rests on nonmilitary considerations, and
the major utility of nuclear weapons is political, then
perhaps negotiations might offer an alternative to the
arms race, especially since most observers agree that
the Soviet threat to Western Europe, while serious, is
not as menacing as it was in the early postwar years.

Initially it should be recognized that both East
and West resist negotiations which would make nuclear
war an unacceptable extension of political influence.
If one is an American, to abandon any means to the
eventual victory over communism is to encourage moral
disarmament. Such fatalism, it is said, can only
result in a Soviet takeover without a fight: better
Red than dead. If one is a Soviet citizen, such
thinking undermines the rationale for large military
expenditures which are providing the means to hold the
line against Fascist Imperialistic Capitalism. This
propensity to remain faithful to von Clausewitz's
notion that war is but an extension of politics by
other means, even in a nuclear age, creates a serious
military as well as political and moral problem.

At the same time, it must be admitted that the
pursuit of security through the modernization and
expansion of nuclear weapons, especially in space, has
become in itself a threat to peace. For every new
technological innovation, there is a countermeasure.
To escape requires a broader focus taking into account
the full spectrum of historical, social, economic, and

political forces, but at the same time recognizing the
necessity to concentrate on nuclear weapons and arms
control without permitting a linkage to every other
conceivable East-West international problem. It may be
necessary to question the assumptions of the political
realists and the adequacy of deterrence theory as a way
of understanding international relations.

Yet the nuclear weapon, more than any other single
factor, has determined the way the United States and
the Soviet Union have defined their post-World War II
interests (Sonnenfeldt, p. 6). There are those who do
not shrink from nuclear war and are comfortable with
"war-fighting" strategies. It is true that both
Soviet and American leaders recognize the qualitatively
new character of these double-edged weapons, but there
is a tendency to think of them as just more powerful
conventional explosives. This leads to the development
of strategies for fighting a limited nuclear war which
can be controlled until an "unacceptable level of
damage" is reached, whereupon the game will be called
off. Certainly this is to place too much confidence in
man's rationality under conditions of stress. It seems
almost certain that a tactical nuclear war would
immediately lead to the destruction of Europe and in
short order to an all-out nuclear exchange that would
destroy both the Soviets and the Americans.

The danger of nuclear war is clearly one of the
major threats to the national interest of all countries
and should be a paramount concern to leaders and
followers alike. Instead we find apathy on the part of
the public and cynicism on the part of the leadership.
Reducing the dangers of nuclear war is serious
business, but whether security rests in the clenched
fist or the open palm is a matter of debate.

According to the U.S. Department of Defense, the
primary goal of arms control within the framework of
deterrence theory is stability.

> The United States is committed to an arms
> control process that, if it were to lead to
> equitable and verifiable agreements, could
> strengthen deterrence and enhance stability
> while radically reducing the numbers and
> destructive power of Soviet and American
> nuclear weapons. (Soviet Military Power,
> p. 144)

In the Introduction to this volume, General
Seignious also stressed the importance of stability as
the primary goal of arms control. Ambassador Adelman
has said that we will continue to pursue meaningful,
equitable, and verifiable agreements (Adelman, p. 441).
The concepts of political equilibrium and military
stability are most appealing to status quo powers;
however, in a nuclear-armed world they have much to
recommend themselves as ways of preserving all mankind.

THE GOAL OF STABILITY

Despite the paramount importance of stability, many U.S. and Soviet weapons systems are destabilizing: the Soviet SS-20s because they are the first theater nuclear weapons to threaten European capitals, the United States Pershing II missiles because they almost require the Soviets to "launch on warning," the rail-mobile Soviet SS-X-24 because of its counterforce capability, the United States MX missile because it is such a tempting target, and on both sides cruise missiles because those with nuclear warheads are indistinguishable from those without, thus complicating the verification problems.

The Strategic Defense Initiative (SDI) may also be destabilizing. If SDI is intended to strengthen nuclear deterrence by providing the cover to make American ICBMs invulnerable rather than providing a shift to a defensive posture for American cities, it inevitably will be perceived as threatening by the Soviets. "Star Wars," ostensibly a defensive system, is likely to encourage the Soviets to multiply the number of their offensive weapons to insure that some will get through. Even so, if SDI were to provide a protective shield to second-strike weapons, such as Midgetman, it could contribute to stability. Just as the ocean provides invulnerability for the American nuclear-powered submarines, SDI could guarantee the protection of second-strike weapons. However, if SDI provides protection for the United States, while the Soviets continue to be highly vulnerable, the Soviets will, no doubt, consider this as representing a substantial shift in the balance of power.

If stability is an important goal, then the deployment of new weapons cannot be initiated without taking into account how the other side will react. If the reaction is to increase the number of weapons, to shorten the response time, and to make verification difficult or impossible, the development of these new weapons does not lead to the stated U.S. and Soviet goal of military stability but instead to its opposite--a rapidly escalating arms race.

THE GOAL OF EQUALITY

Historically, the United States and the Soviet Union have been militarily in a position of inferiority relative to other European nation-states. The emergence of the United States as a global superpower after World War II was first accepted with reluctance. More recently the United States has become accustomed to its position as "leader of the free world," a role which the Soviets, believing that the future of the world has been entrusted to them, feel obligated to challenge.

When the Soviet Union moved from a position of military inferiority vis-a-vis the United States to one of equality in the late sixties, this shift in the balance of power was difficult for the United States to accept. It has long been known that the strong are inclined to do what they please, the weak suffer what they must. To reject nuclear superiority as a goal and substitute essential equivalence goes against the grain, especially for a state which has only recently attained that position and is not sensitive to the dangers of hubris and the arrogance of power which has been the downfall of so many.

The individualistic competitiveness of American character makes it difficult to accept equality unless it is interpreted as an equal opportunity to get ahead. It seems from the negotiating record that the Reagan Administration is more comfortable with a policy of superiority than one of parity despite its lip service to the latter. The contradictory voices within the Administration make it difficult to evaluate the recent transition to a negotiating posture and away from a position that was hostile to arms control talks.

Another difficulty with the concept of equality of American and Soviet military weapons systems is that comparability across the "spectrum of risk" is practically impossible to determine because of the asymmetry of forces and the complexity of measuring the strength of nuclear weapons. Certainly equality does not mean that we should match the Soviets tank for tank. Equality should not imply a need to maintain a counterforce strategy which selectively targets military installations so that a "controlled" war-fighting capacity is possible. If both sides are equally capable of destroying the other, that should be sufficient to deter a first strike. Maintaining a meaningful military balance or equality is essential for security, but excessive nuclear weapons are counterproductive.

Arms control offers one way to maintain parity, but it is not a panacea. SALT I made progress in limiting the number of launchers, but no weapons were dismantled, no nuclear subs mothballed, and no missile silos vacated. The number of weapons has steadily increased despite the existing arms control treaties. On the other hand, we are far safer because there are no nuclear weapons in space, on the ocean floor, or in Antarctica, not to mention the halt to atmospheric testing as a result of the Limited Test Ban Treaty. A major goal of arms control should be not only to maintain parity, but to radically reduce the number and destructive power of these weapons to a safer and more economical level.

THE GOAL OF REDUCTIONS

Another word for "reduction," some critics claim, should be "modernization." Both the Soviets and Americans seem inclined to get rid of only those weapons that are obsolete.

Stability and equality do not necessarily imply reduction, and some authors have even argued that reductions can be destabilizing. If reductions are seen as valuable, one must also ask whether they should be the result of some bold initiative or carefully planned to take place incrementally.

The various proposals for a 50 percent cut in strategic arms have a great deal of popular appeal. Deep reduction in weapons to a level of "minimal deterrence" has been recommended by advocates of the Freeze Movement. Professor George Kennan suggests that some bold reciprocal measures of restraint are required if the problem is to become manageable (Kennan, Nuclear Delusion, p. xxiii); however, supporters of the somewhat neglected Nuclear Build-Down proposal would proceed using more measured steps. General Scowcroft, somewhat skeptical of dramatic reductions without careful consideration for the appropriate mix, has recommended that "we integrate strategic force programs, especially our ICBM programs, with arms control; and then move both in the direction of enhanced stability" (Scowcroft, p. 3). Whether the process is rapid or slow, some reduction would seem rational, given the dangers of nuclear accidents and the economic cost to the civilian sector of maintaining the equilibrium at the highest possible level.

A serious motivation for reduction has long been the recognition of indirect environmental effects of nuclear explosions such as radioactive fallout, the destruction of the stratospheric ozone layer, and the controversial nuclear winter hypothesis. It would seem certain that if we were not killed by the direct effects of a nuclear blast, we would most likely be destroyed by the secondary effects. Carl Sagan argues that a threshold exists at which the climatic catastrophe could be so great that even without any retaliation national suicide is inevitable (Turco, et al.).

Although recent scientific evidence suggests that the idea of automatic suicide is unsupportable, taking into account the largely unknown effects of nuclear war on the environment should make us more aware of the urgent need for reductions in the nuclear arsenal (Thompson and Schneider, p. 1005). The combination of direct and indirect effects on the ecological system makes the consequences of nuclear war incomprehensible. Given the fact that scientists are still mystified by the comparatively simple task of predicting reoccurring weather patterns, it staggers the imagination to think that we could predict with any certainty the consequences of an all-out nuclear exchange.

Regardless of the goals established for reduction of weapons systems, some unintended consequences should be taken into consideration.   Reductions might also encourage horizontal proliferation since some non-nuclear countries would have a better chance of catching up (Thompson and Schneider, p. 1000). Unless reduction is carefully controlled, it can be destabilizing since it might encourage one side or the other to take advantage of some perceived or real temporary weakness and launch a preemptive war.   A shift from reliance on nuclear to conventional weapons might bring about development of alternative biological and chemical weapons or even more terrible weapons as yet undreamed of.   Small numbers of weapons make the verification problem more difficult.   The dangers of an arms race cannot necessarily be alleviated by simply cutting back the cuts must be exercised reciprocally, the mix must be carefully evaluated, and alternative military strategies developed.

This process of reduction is even more precarious when one factors in innovative research which must inevitably be part of the arms control process.   It is unreasonable to think that new technologies will not be developed which will substantially alter the power equation.   A refusal to discuss such technological innovations casts doubt on the commitment to serious efforts to stabilize the military balance.   For example, if one side develops a Strategic Defense Initiative, against attack while modernizing its "first-strike" weapons, it will be perceived as a threat by the other side.   Clearly both sides require such a "shield" if the balance of power is to be maintained.   In the current political climate, a sharing of technology which would make this "dual shield" plan a success seems politically impossible.   A related problem will develop if the NATO countries perceive SDI as decoupling the interests of the United States from European security.   The Strategic Defense Initiative could encourage countries such as France and Great Britian to accelerate their production of nuclear weapons.   Under these circumstances SDI seems anything but an effective, safe, and moral way to prevent war.

Recognizing the difficulties of reducing the number of nuclear weapons does not take away from the need to attack the problem.   Clearly 50,000 nuclear weapons in the world are far more than are needed for any rational military purpose.   The supreme irony is that neither side wants to or intends to use any of these weapons unless placed in a position of extreme danger. In a world where people are starving every day, we are spending billions of dollars for weapons only to reassure ourselves that they will never be used.

THE GOAL OF VERIFICATION

In the past, verification and confirmation problems have inhibited rather than aided arms control solutions. This has been especially true when it comes to intrusive or on-site verification. With the advent of modern surveillance techniques this problem has been greatly reduced, since it is possible to monitor carefully the testing and deployment of nuclear weapons. It is extremely unlikely the Soviets can build a sufficient clandestine capability to threaten U.S. security interests without being detected (Gayler, p. 27).

The two most recent verification problems relative to Soviet military activities concern the encryption of ballistic missile telemetry from Soviet tests and the building of a Soviet radar site at Krasnoyarsk in central Siberia. The low-level encryption currently engaged in by the Soviets apparently is not a serious problem for the National Security Agency analysts; however, it potentially complicates the verification process. The Krasnoyarsk radar site is a more serious violation of at least the spirit of the Anti-Ballistic Missile (ABM) Treaty and has raised serious questions, especially in the U.S. Senate, concerning the confidence which we should have in future arms control negotiations. On-site inspection has been agreed to in principle by the Soviets and should not represent an insurmountable obstacle to further negotiations. A U.S. visit to the controversial Soviet radar site would do a great deal to overcome American fears of cheating.

Verification of the number and disposition of existing weapons systems is difficult, but verification of research into new weapons systems is practically impossible. As Kissinger noted years ago, it is no longer necessary to acquire easily recognizable new territory or additional resources to increase a nation's power (Kissinger, p. 4). Major shifts of power in the modern world are likely to occur in the laboratory. Even though it is difficult to put constraints on research, there is no reason one should not consider limiting testing and deployment of new technologies.

The verification problem, however, is as much symbolic as real. The question is, How can the integrity of the arms control process be protected? If a nation's leaders are to become committed to arms control, they must have assurances that the agreements will be kept and that alleged violations can be reviewed and appropriate action taken to restore compliance. Since international treaties have traditionally been kept only as long as they advance the interests of the nations involved, it is natural, in lieu of clear verification procedures, to be skeptical of whether we can "trust" the Russians and vice versa. Yet it seems reasonable that arms control is in the interest of the Soviets as well as the Americans.   It is mutual interest rather than altruism that forms the foundation of arms control.

THE GOAL OF A MORALLY ACCEPTABLE DEFENSE POLICY

As Kenneth W. Thompson recently pointed out, man often seeks to escape the realities of politics through moralism, utopianism, and the propensity to equate political success with moral superiority (Thompson, pp. 9-11). Political realists have pointed out that moralistic-legalistic approaches to international politics have inherent difficulties. President Reagan has suggested that arms control, an intrinsically moral endeavor, may in fact accelerate the arms race rather than slow it down. The Soviets have used the SALT agreements, he says, as a legalistic cover to build more weapons. Under these circumstances arms control talks are worthless. Recently, Mr. Reagan indicated that further compliance of the United States with the provisions of SALT II may not advance our national interest if the Soviets are not going to comply with the treaties already negotiated. If the United States asserts hostile intent on the part of the Soviets and views them as a demonic force, then negotiations are out of the question.

The United States, it could be argued, has not always negotiated in what some have called the "spirit of Geneva." There has been the specific intent of leaving options open for future military developments. Some cynics say that the price of SALT I was MIRV; the price of SALT II was MX; and the price of the recent negotiations may be SDI. Certainly the fact that the ratification of SALT II by the United States Senate in part fell victim to domestic policies shows how little commitment there is among some of our more important political leaders.

A strong element of political realism as well as idealism has been present in the rhetoric of both East and West and has served both as a way of building political cohesiveness. Idealism has also sometimes served as a rationalization for national self-interest. The Homeric gods may have departed the battlefield, but a strong dose of idealism still may be needed not the pseudo-idealism of the propagandists, but the genuine good will of the statesman. A moralistic outlook which sees the other side as always wrong is dangerous, but a morality grounded in the view that life is good and should be preserved would make a positive contribution to the discussions. There is no reason to think that such a moral precept is not shared by the Soviets as well as the Americans.

Within our own country the American Catholic Bishops are saying that "decisions about nuclear weapons are among the most pressing moral questions of our age" (National Conference of Catholic Bishops,

Challenge, p. vii). They have come very close to
declaring as immoral the policy of nuclear deterrence
and have certainly stated in no uncertain terms that
the use of nuclear weapons is immoral. Nuclear
deterrence, according to the bishops, has not preserved
an equilibrium of forces, but instead has become a
justification for the build-up of nuclear arms. A
strategy of nuclear deterrence is at best a necessary
evil for the short term. If the views of the American
Catholic Bishops are shared by the general population,
a new look should be taken at U.S. defense policy. It
is unlikely that laws and government policies which are
viewed as immoral by a large number of citizens can be
successful.

Not only the established churches, but the Peace
Movement, a kind of secular church, has provided a
moral criticism of the arms race for a large body of
disaffected citizens, many of whom have lost their
sense of church identification. Many peace activists,
although not affiliated with organized religion, retain
a sense of righteous indignation when they consider the
insane consequences of the contemporary nuclear
situation. The Peace Movement utilizes the rhetoric of
religion, such as the impending apocalypse, in its mass
celebrations and calls for action to prevent the forces
of evil from destroying the world. Crusades of any sort
can get out of hand and encourage simplistic solutions
to complex problems, but despite the inability of mass
movements to cope with the intricacies of arms control,
the appearance of 500,000 peace marchers tends to focus
the attention of political leaders on the problem and
to dramatize a serious moral issue.

The anomalies, contradictions, and paradoxes
inherent in nuclear deterrence theory should be
sufficient to force a re-evaluation of our assumptions
and to generate a search for a new paradigm to explain
international politics in an age armed with nuclear
weapons. It is necessary to move outside the box of
nuclear deterrence theory and develop an alternative
defense policy. Echoing Albert Einstein's famous
statement that "we shall require a substantially new
manner of thinking if mankind is to survive," the
bishops claim that the policy itself is seriously
flawed and must be rethought before progress can be
made in reducing nuclear weapons. Paul Ramsey, in a
recent article entitled "Farewell to Christian
Realism," states that we first define an action as
"intolerably evil in itself" or "morally intolerable"
and then make ready to perform it under certain
circumstances (Ramsey, p. 479). He calls for not only
a rethinking of the policy of Mutual Assured
Destruction (MAD) but a review of the adequacy of
political realism as a framework for understanding
national security. Even if we are unwilling to
abandon the assumptions of political realism, a defense
policy designed to cope with the nuclear dilemma that
relies on the threat of unleashing such ultimate

destruction is unacceptable over the long haul to civilized people. Protecting Western civilization by destroying Western civilization is irrational.

Being ever mindful of the Machiavellian injunction that some things which appear to be good are in fact bad, and some things which appear to be bad are in fact good, it is time to rethink nuclear deterrence theory as adequate for national security. In the meantime, for practical and moral reasons arms control negotiations are important. Arms control agreements, both tacit and explicit, offer the hope that the dangers of nuclear war can be reduced incrementally at least until an alternative military strategy can be developed. It is perhaps the best short-term hope for survival, but it clearly will not be effective without a sense of commitment that avoids appeal to moralistic utopian sentiments and to the ethnocentric egos of the superpowers. It is sometimes useful to "see ourselves as others see us," and it is clear that in spite of the military strength of the two superpowers, they are not viewed as morally superior by the rest of the world, and, for example, are seen by many Muslim leaders as having similar (immoral) plans for imperial expansion (Pipes, p. 939).

CONCLUSION

Arms control negotiations, although complicated by the problems inherent in the concepts of equality, reduction, and verification, still offer some hope of managing the arms race in the short term and reducing the number of nuclear weapons to a level which can only be used to deter nuclear attack while we search for a moral alternative to Mutual Assured Destruction. It is essential to remember that these weapons are potential agents of catastrophic devastation, and all mankind shares a real interest, political, economic, and otherwise, in bringing them under control. This awareness should bring the necessary commitment to the task and make it possible to resolve the technical difficulties and to see beyond the too easily accepted metaphors of the time. The goal should be to at first reduce nuclear weapons to a level consistent with providing "minimal deterrence," and then to ban all nuclear weapons worldwide. More important than the technical problems of specific arms control talks is the development of a sense of political vision which transcends the absurd situation we have created. The problem is not so much the survival of an individual. Let's face it, most of us have only a few years to live in any event, but the survival of civilization and perhaps the survival of the human species is at stake.

PART 2

U.S. and Soviet Nuclear Weapons Policy

5

Nuclear Weapons Policy of the USSR

Raymond L. Garthoff

Nuclear weapons policy, of course, is inseparable from defense policy, foreign policy, arms control policy, and the basic national security policy of any country. This is evident in the many facets that it has, and it is equally true of countries such as the Soviet Union with its ideology. While Marxism-Leninism is predicated on a conflict among contending classes, and since 1917 among contending states, it is not one in which the primary place is given to military power. Military power is recognized as one essential and element in international political life, but it is not seen as the driving force of history. So, to the extent that the Soviets are driven by ideological imperatives, this leads them to expect that the historical process, a progressive revolutionary change in society, is what is going to change the world.

THE EVOLUTION OF SOVIET NUCLEAR POLICY

The historical evolution of Soviet military policy has coincided with the nuclear age. The Soviet Union began its nuclear weapons development program in highest secrecy almost exactly at the same time as the United States in 1940. They interrupted it to meet more immediate wartime needs in 1941 and 1942, but by 1943 they were back with their own Manhattan project. One result was that the first Soviet atomic explosion occurred in 1949, only four years after ours, and well before it had been expected by the American government. The Soviets remained behind in the development of nuclear weapons for some time, however.

Initially, in the early postwar period, Stalin seemed to speak disparagingly about atomic weapons. This was not because he was uninformed, but because it made perfectly good sense to take that position at a time when the Soviet Union first had no nuclear weapons and then had relatively few. For domestic morale and political purposes, and for international political purposes, he did not want to lend more weight to a

weapon which his opponent had and which he did not.
But the Soviets were certainly aware of the importance
of nuclear weapons, and became more so (as did we)
during the 1950s and 1960s.

From 1954 through 1959 nuclear weapons were
essentially integrated into traditional Soviet military
doctrine. They tend to think in terms of a World War
II with nuclear weapons added, not very different from
the concepts of "broken-back war" prevalent in this
country in much of the 1950s as well. A considerable
change occurred in the Soviet Union in 1959-60 when
Nikita Khrushchev pushed a debate among the military.
We became later very well informed about this debate
thanks to a tremendous amount of highly classified
Soviet material which was provided by Colonel Oleg
Penkovsky, a Soviet officer who became a spy for the
United States. The view which Khrushchev pushed
contended that nuclear weapons had changed everything,
and that one didn't need large armies, navies, and air
forces in the nuclear age.

There was strong opposition to this view within
the military establishment, and during the early 1960s
a compromise was duly effected that included the
recognition that while a nuclear war might be short and
all-destructive, it might also be protracted and
require substantial conventional military power in
addition to an initial nuclear exchange. Overall,
however, military doctrine in the early half of the
1960s developed in terms of a clear assumption that any
war between the Soviet Union and the United States,
between the East and West, would be a war to the end
between the two systems and an all-out nuclear war.

AVOIDING NUCLEAR WAR

During the latter 1960s an important change took
place.   Recognizing that nuclear war would be in fact
so destructive that neither side under any
circumstance, including an attack by surprise, would be
able to prevail in any meaningful sense, the Soviets
decided that if at all possible nuclear war must be
avoided. That decision was made not because of any
intrinsically pacific interest, but because of a very
hard-headed calculation of what the consequences of a
nuclear war would be. So they changed their military
doctrine to put more emphasis on preparing for the
contingency of a non-nuclear war.

They considered questions of possible limited use
of nuclear weapons, but although they did not
necessarily preclude a response in a limited nuclear
way, they were not attracted to limited nuclear war
options. While the threshold definitely has been
between nuclear and non-nuclear war, they have
preferred to keep any war that might occur non-nuclear,
for if it did become nuclear it would almost certainly

become an all-out war and destroy the Soviet Union. When they changed their military doctrine and structure, they restored a good deal of the conventional artillery that they had reduced drastically in the early 1960s, and in many other ways began to rebuild a greater capability for non-nuclear war.   These steps were taken to meet the contingency of keeping a war non-nuclear, no matter how it might begin. Among the things that contributed to this change at that time was a recognition of prospective nuclear parity with the United States. They had not achieved it yet, but it was coming, they were catching up. Another reason was the evident awareness in the West also of the disadvantages of nuclear war and, therefore, the possibility that the West would also cooperate in its interests in keeping a non-nuclear war from escalating. We expressed this as the doctrine of flexible response. This also encouraged them to consider a similar flexible response position on their own side.

BALLISTIC MISSILE DEFENSE

These changes also coincided with or contributed to a debate in the late 1960s over the question of ballistic missile defense, a subject which is again back in the forefront. Also, at that particular juncture the United States had proposed what eventually became SALT. Our initial proposal had been for an agreement to head off a race in anti-ballistic missile systems, or ABM. It was this background of internal doctrinal military and political re-evaluation in the Soviet Union which led to their decision to join the United States in the ABM treaty in 1972.

This was the first time that arms control began to play an important role and the first time the Soviets began to feel that it might be an instrument of policy along with unilateral military programs. The Soviets have not (nor have we) conceived of arms control simply as a goal in itself. It is an instrument of policy and it may be a useful one. The interesting and important thing is that the Soviets began to recognize that it was a possible instrument of policy along with other measures.

STRATEGIC MILITARY PARITY

Let me now discuss briefly the very important period of the 1970s, especially in terms of the way the Soviet Union viewed the developing balance between nuclear weapons and arms control. Unfortunately, in a way, the United States and the Soviet Union in effect agreed at the time of SALT I on the principle of parity between the two sides. This was unfortunate not because it was not a wise thing for the two countries

to do, but because it occurred at a time when the
Soviet Union had not acquired parity. They knew that
very well, and we did too, but it was not generally or
widely understood. The main result of that agreement
was that as the Soviet Union continued in the 1970s,
within the framework of the SALT agreement, to build up
its strategic military power to acquire real parity,
the general impression here, of course, was that there
was something wrong; while we were standing still, the
Soviets were moving ahead to break parity and gain
superiority. This was not really the case, and
certainly not the way it looked in Moscow.

Let us look at what did happen during the 1970s.
Often it has been said that this was a period of
relentless and unprecedented build-up of Soviet
strategic power. Well it was very impressive and
extensive, but it was not unprecedented. In the five
years before the missile levels were capped by the SALT
I agreement, the Soviets had added 1,050 ICBM and SLBM
launchers to their force, which had been very small at
the beginning of that period. But in the preceding
five-year period, the United States had added 1,060
ICBM and SLBM launchers to its force. We built up
sooner and then we leveled off. Then they caught up
and went a little beyond us in terms of the total
number, especially of ICBM launchers. They had,
however, 300 of those oriented and directed against
targets on the Eurasian Periphery, so in absolute terms
the numbers were not as disparate as they seemed in the
SALT I interim agreement figures. The important thing
is that by that time the number of launchers did not
really matter much, because the United States had moved
the competition into the number of warheads.

At the beginning of 1970 we were deploying MIRVed
warheads on ICMBs and SLBMs. This was five years
before the first Soviet operational deployment of
MIRVs. They then moved into a substantial buildup in
the late 1970s of their own MIRVed systems. If one
looks at it that way, the absolute increase in number
of warheads during that period was, indeed, larger on
the Soviet side. Since, however, we were adding at
such a substantial pace, the American total at the end
of the decade remained significantly larger than the
first Soviet total. To this day, we have a larger
number of warheads in our operational strategic forces,
although the numbers are very close and hardly a matter
of significant calibration when we are talking about
10,000 warheads on each side.

Other Administration spokesmen have recently noted
the fact that by comparison with the situation in the
1960s, megatonage of our forces and the number of
warheads are down. What is not always understood is
that those changes took place in the 1960's, and for
the reason that we moved from a very large bomber
force, with a very large number of very large bombs,
into the missile era. We reduced our megatonage mainly
because we moved B-52s from high-altitude delivery,

where the standard munition was a 20-megaton bomb, to one-megaton bombs with higher accuracy and equal value for destroying military targets. That is why our megatonage went down, and it happened before the competition of the 1970s even began. The same is true for the number of warheads, including bombs in this case. So if one looks at the competition from 1970 on, one sees a picture quite different from the rather irrelevant description of what we unilaterally did in the 1960s to adjust to the Soviet nuclear "threat."

ASATS: ANTI-SATELLITE SYSTEMS

An example of another different "picture" is the Soviet development of an anti-satellite system (ASAT), which is now considered to have been operational by 1971. It is not as often mentioned that the United States deployed an operational anti-satellite system in 1963. I remember this very well because I happened, I confess, to have been one of the drafters of recommendation for it that President Kennedy approved. In 1963 we deployed an operational anti-satelitte system at Kwajalein Island based on the Nike-Zeus system. From 1964 until 1975 we had an operational anti-satellite deployment at Johnston Island in the Pacific. We know from a classified Soviet general staff journal that has since become openly available, that they were very concerned about this development. Although the system remained on a standby status, they counted it as operational, and were very much aware that we had programs underway for more advanced anti-satellite systems. In any event, they started testing in 1968 and concluded a first batch of tests in 1971.

In 1977 Harold Brown, Secretary of Defense, stated that we considered the Soviets to have an operational ASAT. The Reagan Administration in 1981 decided that operational capability should be dated from 1971. The Soviets say they don't have an operational anti-satellite system. Actually, both statements might be true. There is no indication that the Soviets have an operational unit. The Soviet system is a satellite fired from a large booster on an open pad into orbit, which will subsequently intersect with a satellite's orbit and intercept it.

This system, which the Soviets tested from 1968 through 1971 and again occasionally between 1976 and 1982, was not very effective. It took usually a couple of orbits to come into proper contact. They tried testing the system with a better homing arrangement, but that system has not worked well at all. From the Soviet standpoint, in other words, their ASAT system looks different from the way it is perceived here.

In sum, an examination of the present situation and future prospects show that the Soviets are continuing to maintain a very large military force with a wide range of capabilities to meet various contingencies. During the 1970s, they came to believe that they have a useful and important role to play in arms control. Now, in the early 1980s, Moscow seems to be asking not whether strategic arms control is desirable but whether it is obtainable. The United States has not ratified any of the three arms control treaties that it has signed since 1974, the threshold test ban, the peaceful nuclear explosions ban, and, of course, SALT II, and this has certainly put arms control into a more uncertain situation.

We are now seeking to open a dialogue on SDI, which represents a reopening of a dialogue that was held both between the two sides in Moscow in the late 1960s, as discussed above. I personally think that we had it right then, and that SDI is both destabilizing and undesirable. It is, however, the position that the President and his administration have taken. Regrettably, it is clear that as long as the United States keeps up its efforts to develop strategic defenses, the Soviet Union will keep open its options for offensive systems to assure it retaliatory deterrent capability, and there will be no offensive arms reductions.

REFERENCES

Garthoff, Raymond L., Detente and Confrontation: American Soviet Relations from Nixon to Reagan (Washington, D. C.: Brookings Institution, 1985).

Garthoff, Raymond L., Perspectives on the Strategic Balance (Washington, D. C.: Brookings Institution, 1983).

Green, William C., Soviet Nuclear Weapons Policy: Research Guide (Boulder, Colo.: Westview Press, 1986).

Holloway, David, The Soviet Union and the Arms Race (New Haven, Conn.: Yale University Press, 1983).

Laird, Robbin R., and Dale R. Herspring, The Soviet Union and Strategic Arms (Boulder, Colo.: Westview Press, 1984).

6

The Policy of The United States on Nuclear Weapons, 1945–1985

Larry H. Addington

The American policy on nuclear weapons was first set in 1942 when President Franklin D. Roosevelt made the decision to proceed with the Manhattan Project in order to develop an atomic weapon before the end of World War II. His motivation was to foreclose the possibility that Nazi Germany might develop and monopolize such a weapon in time to affect the outcome of the war. But before the Manhattan Project could come to fruition with a successful test of the nuclear device Trinity in July 1945, Roosevelt had died, Germany had surrendered, and President Harry S. Truman was faced with the decision as to how the atomic bomb should be used to shorten the war with Japan. Advised by a committee of soldiers, scientists, and statesmen that, for maximum shock effect, the bomb should be used against a major Japanese population center, Truman concurred with the recommendation in hopes of eliminating the need for a costly and prolonged invasion of the Japanese home islands.

The sequel is well known. A plutonium bomb and an untested uranium fission bomb were shipped to a B-29 bomber base in the Pacific. On 6 August 1945, the B-29 "Enola Gay" dropped the uranium bomb on Hiroshima, and on 9 August another B-29 destroyed Nagasaki with the plutonium bomb. Each of the two bombs exploded with the equivalent force of approximately twenty thousand tons of TNT (20 KT), and between them they probably killed 125,000 people outright and caused the eventual deaths of perhaps as many as 300,000 people. The destruction of the two cities, combined with a Soviet declaration of war on Japan between the two atomic bombings, had the desired effect. On 14 August, Japan accepted Allied terms for an armistice, and 2 September the Imperial Japanese government formally surrendered.

FACTORS AFFECTING AMERICAN NUCLEAR WEAPONS POLICY

In the euphoria of victory just after World War
II, the United States attempted to establish
international control over atomic energy through the
United Nations, but with the onset of the Cold War with
the Soviet Union that effort failed. Given the
dramatic role of the atomic bomb in ending the war with
Japan, the United States acted logically in 1947 when
it decided to make the atomic bomb the centerpiece of
its postwar defense policy. But though the United
States still had a monopoly on the secrets of the bomb
at that time, atomic bomb production had ceased with
the end of the Second World War and in early 1947 the
country's entire atomic armory consisted of just two
atomic bombs and the unassembled components for two
more. In addition, the predicted production rate of an
average of fifty bombs per year for the indefinite
future meant that the Pentagon's desire for a minimum
of four hundred bombs could not be reached before the
middle of the 1950s at the earliest.
In the meantime, a number of other factors
influenced American policy on nuclear weapons. In
August 1949, the Soviets successfully tested a fission
weapon similar to that which had destroyed Hiroshima,
and the American monopoly in atomic weapons was broken.
Even more disturbing was the belief that the Soviets
were aggressively pursuing research on a still more
powerful hydrogen or thermonuclear fusion device. In
January 1950, President Truman signed an executive
order committing the United States to develop a fusion
bomb before the Soviet Union could do so. Such a
device was tested in the Pacific in November 1952. It
produced an explosion equivalent to ten million tons of
TNT (10 MT), and was five hundred times more powerful
than the Hiroshima bomb. But hardly had the United
States congratulated itself on the development of the
so-called hydrogen or H-bomb than the Soviet Union
tested one of its own in August 1953. During the rest
of the 1950s, the USSR and the USA competed furiously
in adding more and more fusion and fission weapons to
their armories.
Still another factor that influenced the American
policy on nuclear weapons was the outbreak of the
Korean War in June 1950. The Truman administration
responded to that crisis with a limited remobilization
of conventional forces and research on tactical atomic
weapons suitable for the battlefield. In January 1953,
the month in which President Dwight D. Eisenhower
succeeded Harry S. Truman in office, the U.S. Army
successfully test-fired an atomic shell from a 280mm
cannon that burst with the force of two thousand tons
of TNT (2 KT), or about a tenth of the force of the
Hiroshima bomb. In March 1953, the Joint Chiefs of
Staff urged Eisenhower to consider use of the tactical
nuclear weapon in order to break the stalemate in
Korea. Though Eisenhower used only the threat of

atomic weapons in Korea, and the war was ended through negotiation in July 1953 without their employment, Eisenhower's post-Korea defense policy placed heavy emphasis on tactical, theater, and strategic nuclear weapons for every contingency. The direction in which the United States policy on nuclear weapons was moving was made clear as early as 1954 when John Foster Dulles, Eisenhower's Secretary of State, declared that in future his government reserved the right to respond to "aggression" on any level by "retaliating massively" with weapons of its own choice and at places of its own choosing. "Massive Retaliation" remained the hallmark of US nuclear weapons policy throughout Eisenhower's two terms in office.

But the Soviet Union was also making rapid progress on a variety of nuclear fronts. Though the USSR lagged behind the United States by a large margin in the production of long-range bombers during the 1950s, the Soviets accumulated a growing supply of tactical atomic weapons and developed intermediate-range ballistic missiles (IRBMs) that posed an increasing threat to America's allies in Europe. Even American complacency about the relative invulnerability of the continental United States to Soviet atomic attack was shaken in 1957 when, years ahead of prediction, the USSR carried out a full-range test of an intercontinental ballistic missile (ICBM). The Soviet demonstration led to a crash program by the Eisenhower administration to close the so-called "Missile Gap," and by the time John F. Kennedy entered the White House in January 1961, the United States had more ICBMs deployed than the Soviet Union. In addition, the United States had taken the lead in nuclear-powered, ballistic-missile submarines (SSNBs), each of which could launch sixteen Polaris ballistic missiles against targets in the USSR. The first of a fleet of forty-one SSNBs became operational in December 1960.

THE DEVELOPMENT OF THE TRIAD

Despite the growing distractions of the Vietnam War, first Kennedy and then President Lyndon Johnson saw to the completion of the deployment of the American strategic forces planned in the late 1950s and early 1960s. In 1968, the last of 1,054 Air Force ICBMs was installed in its underground launch-silo within the United States. A thousand of the US ICBMs were of the solid-fuel Minuteman type, the rest liquid-fuel Titans. Also that year the United States launched its forty-first Polaris-armed SSNB, bringing the total of submarine-launched ballistic missiles (SLBMs) to 656. The B-47 bomber had been retired from service in 1965, but 520 jet-engined B-52s completed the so-called "Triad" of American strategic forces. The Soviet strategic forces in 1968 amounted to 850 ICBMs, 40

SLBMs, and 155 bombers. But whereas American expansion of numbers of strategic nuclear carriers ceased after 1968, Soviets expansion continued, especially in heavy, land-based ICBMs. By 1970 the number of Soviet ICBMs had grown to 1,300, and by 1972 to about 1,500. By 1972 in the United States, 550 of the 1,000 Minuteman ICBMs had been MIRVed (i.e., equipped with multiple, independently-targetable nuclear warheads), and the single-warhead Polaris had been replaced by the MIRVed Poseidon SLBM; however, no new strategic bombers had been added to the American "Triad," and the aging B-52s were declining in numbers. In addition, the asymetrical nature of the US and Soviet nuclear armories made a comparison of their relative strengths increasingly difficult. Still, it was clear by 1972, if not before, that if each side could actually deliver the nuclear firepower it possessed, the result would approach total destruction for both sides.

THE RECOGNITION OF MUTUAL VULNERABILITY

As early as 1961, the Kennedy administration had concluded that the use of an atomic weapon was so fraught with the danger of escalation to nuclear holocaust that it replaced the Eisenhower policy of "Massive Retaliation" with one of "Flexible Response." Stripped to its essentials, the new policy called for greater emphasis on conventional defense and the making of atomic weapons the last, rather than the first, line of defense.

This trend in U.S. nuclear weapons policy was reinforced during the administration of Lyndon Johnson when discouraging experiments with Anti-Ballistic Missiles (ABMs) led Robert S. McNamara, Secretary of Defense, to conclude that there was no effective active defense against Soviet ICBMs except the threat of retaliation. Despite a Soviet ABM system deployed around Moscow, the USSR was judged to be as vulnerable to strategic nuclear attack as the United States. McNamara believed that additional strategic offensive forces on either side would not appreciably change this situation, and that a finite number of weapons, provided they were invulnerable to preemptive attack, would be sufficient for deterring Soviet nuclear attack on the United States in the foreseeable future. Given these developments and assumptions, in the late 1960s the United States began a shift to a new doctrine called Mutual Assured Destruction (MAD), and sought through bilateral negotiations to cap the strategic arms race with the USSR. The first Strategic Arms Limitation Treaty (SALT I) was signed in 1972 during the Nixon administration, and the second treaty (SALT II) was signed in 1979 during the Carter administration.

ARMS CONTROL NEGOTIATIONS AND THE NATO ALLIANCE

While SALT II was still being negotiated during the latter half of the 1970s, an unexpected complication resulted from the growing uncertainty whether the US strategic deterrent was still linked to the defense of Western Europe. If a mutual exchange of strategic systems would devastate both the USA and the USSR, then would the United States run the risk of committing suicide by retaliating for a Soviet attack on Western Europe? West German Chancellor Helmuth Schmidt voiced this concern while making a speech to the Institute for Strategic Studies in London in September 1977. In that speech, he implied that SALT was having the unintended effect of gradually "decoupling" Western Europe's defense from that of the United States. Of the European members of the North Atlantic Treaty Organization (NATO), only Britain and France had their own nuclear deterrent forces; the remaining European members of NATO, including West Germany, were entirely dependent on the United States. Schmidt's concern was increased by the growing Soviet deployment of the SS-20 IRBM, a MIRVed system with greater range and striking power than the Soviet IRBMs deployed in the 1950s. He implied that West Europeans would not be reassured with anything less than a similar American missile force in Europe.

President Jimmy Carter's administration eventually reacted to Schmidt's concerns by proposing the deployment of 572 Pershing II ballistic and Tomahawk cruise missiles in Western Europe beginning in December 1983. The NATO Council approved the proposal, but on condition that none of the new weapons would be deployed before Theater-Range Nuclear Force (TNF) negotiations were undertaken with the USSR. The Carter administration accepted the so-called "Two-Track Missile Strategy" (i.e., of negotiating while preparing to deploy), but in December 1979 the USSR jeopardized both the strategy and Senatorial ratification of SALT II by intervening in the civil war in Afghanistan. In retaliation for the Soviet action in Afghanistan, Carter withdrew SALT II from the Senate's consideration (though he maintained an informal observance of its terms), and during the rest of his tenure gave more attention to rearmament than to further negotiations with the Soviets.

THE REAGAN APPROACH

After Ronald Reagan's administration took office in January 1981, the momentum of the slide away from the assumptions of MAD, and a reduction in the reliance on arms-control treaties increased . The Reagan administration's defense theorists believed that the United States had fallen behind the USSR militarily, and Reagan was determined to press the build-up of strategic forces before seriously negotiating with the

USSR again. Moreover, he implicitly rejected the idea
that the United States could not be effectively
defended from Soviet ballistic missiles when, in March
1983, he proposed the Strategic Defense Initiative
(SDI). This so-called "Star Wars" proposal called for
space-based defensive weapons capable of destroying
Soviet ICBMs or their warheads after launch. Though
such a system was years away from deployment, even its
proposal marked an important change in the U.S. policy
on nuclear weapons.

In fulfilment of Carter's pledge in December 1979,
Reagan commenced the so-called Intermediate-Range
Nuclear Force (INF) talks in the fall of 1981, and, on
his own initiative, Reagan launched the Strategic Arms
Reduction Talks (START), also held in Geneva, in June
1982. But in the INF talks the Reagan delegation never
formally offered any plan except for one calling for
complete dismantlement of the Soviet SS-20 force in
return for non-deployment of the Pershing and Tomahawk,
the so-called "Zero-Zero Option" rejected out of hand
by the Soviet government and even privately criticized
by the head of the American INF delegation. Further,
Reagan's deployment of the first batteries of Pershing
II and Tomahawk missiles in Western Europe in November
1983 resulted in the Soviets walking out of both the
INF and the START negotiations. The year 1984 was
memorable for being the first in many years in which no
bilateral nuclear weapon negotiations took place
between the United States and the Soviet Union.
Meanwhile, the strategic arms race, only modestly
abated by informal observance of the SALT II
limitations, continued.

After Reagan's reelection in November 1984,
nuclear arms negotiations began anew at Geneva in March
1985. Though Reagan has gone out of his way to warn
against the expectation of early results in the renewed
nuclear arms negotiations, the pressures of an
imbalanced budget - Reagan's deficit of $750 billion
over four years dwarfed the $45 billion of the Carter
administration - and growing Congressional
disenchantment with handing out blank checks to a
Pentagon increasingly perceived as wasteful, may
combine to bring about a new direction in U.S. nuclear
weapons policy.

CONCLUSION

This discussion of American nuclear weapons policy
over the last forty years has tried to emphasize the
following points. First, the policy has as its
cornerstone a belief that the United States must have
equality, if not superiority, in any "winning weapon"
over any actual or potential enemy, and secondly, the
policy is undergirded by the belief that possession of
such weapons confers greater security to the United
States and its allies than any military or diplomatic

alternative. But under the U.S. nuclear weapons policy
of the last forty years, the deterrent value of atomic
weapons has been stressed more than their actual use.
Thus far, the United States has waged its wars since
World War II with non-atomic forces. However, there
has always been an implicit struggle between the policy
makers for whom atomic weapons represent the option of
last resort and only under the most catastrophic
conditions, and those for whom atomic weapons represent
an option of first resort and in a variety of
situations. The debate between advocates of "last use"
and advocates of "first use" remains in the background
of all current debates on U.S. nuclear weapons policy.
Finally, the American penchant for seeking in
technology a means of solving all of its defense
problems has, in the case of the Reagan administration,
extended to defensive systems against nuclear attack.
In reality, nuclear weapons are not likely to be
abolished or neutralized by the SDI, or by any other
technological innovation for that matter, and, short of
a renewed American commitment to the treaty approach,
the American policy on nuclear arms, like its Soviet
counterpart, is likely to continue to fuel the arms
race.

REFERENCES

Cox, Arthur Macy. Russian Roulette: The Superpower
    Game. New York: Times Books, 1982.

Feis, Herbert. Japan Subdued: The Atomic Bomb and
    the End of the War in the Pacific. Princeton:
    Princeton University Press, 1961

Herken, Gregg. Counsels of War. New York: Alfred
    A. Knopf, 1985.

-------------. The Winning Weapon: The Atomic Bomb
    in the Cold War, 1945-1950. New York: Alfred A.
    Knopf, 1980.

Hollway, David. The Soviet Union and the Arms Race.
    New Haven and London: Yale University Press,
    1983.

Prados, John. The Soviet Estimate: U.S. Intelligence
    Analysis and Russian Military Strength. New York:
    Dial Press, 1982.

Talbott, Strobe. Deadly Gambits: The Reagan
    Administration and the Stalemate in Nuclear Arms
    Control. New York: Alfred A. Knopf, 1984.

--------------. Endgame: The Inside Story of SALT
    II. New York: Harper Colophon Books, 1980.

Weigley, Russell F. The American Way of War: A
    History of United States Military Strategy and
    Policy. New York and London: Macmillan, 1973.

Wyden, Peter. Day One: Before Hiroshima and After.
    New York: Simon and Schuster, 1984.

7

NATO, Nuclear Weapons, and Arms Control

Edward B. Davis

The North Atlantic Treaty Organization (NATO) has had a nuclear capability since its creation through the contribution of the various nuclear forces of the United States. This has been supplemented by the British nuclear force, which has been under NATO direction since 1963, as well as by the independent French nuclear force, which would probably be available in a war with the Soviet Union. The possession and planned use of this NATO nuclear capability has had, and continues to have, a major impact on arms control efforts in the European theater as well as at the strategic level.

These arms control efforts constitute an integral part of NATO's overall nuclear strategy. Not only does NATO attempt to develop and deploy nuclear and conventional forces designed to provide a deterrent, but it also wishes, at the same time, to limit Soviet and Warsaw Pact deployments of new weapons which might threaten to overwhelm NATO defenses.

NATO was founded in 1949 to counter the threat of expansion into Western Europe by the Soviet Union. This followed the consolidation of the Soviet presence in Eastern Europe, the coup in Czechoslovakia in 1948, and the growing tension between the USSR and the Western allies as illustrated by, among other examples, the Berlin airlift. This threat was perceived as one which was beyond the defensive capabilities of the Europeans themselves and which could only be balanced with the addition of American military forces. The willingness of the United States to enter a peacetime alliance in Europe marked a dramatic reversal of its traditional diplomatic posture and its recognition that it could no longer exist in isolation from the rest of the world.

With the United States as a founding member, NATO had a nuclear capability from the beginning because the United States extended its strategic nuclear umbrella to cover Europe. Later, the United States introduced theater nuclear forces in Europe in order to enhance its deterrent capability in the area. These theater nuclear forces ranged from Atomic Demolition Munitions and other short-range battlefield weapons to longer-range systems. An important step in this development was the meeting in December 1957, when the NATO Heads of Government decided that it was necessary to establish stocks of nuclear warheads in Europe and that Intermediate Range Ballistic Missiles (IRBMs) should be placed at the disposal of the Supreme Allied Commander Europe (SACEUR). The United States immediately sent sixty Thor IRBMs to the United Kingdom under a dual-key system, and later sent others to Italy and Turkey. This decision came after the 1955 accession of the Federal Republic of Germany to NATO, which allowed the alliance to extend formally its Forward Strategy (adopted in September 1950) to that country. Thus, NATO would meet any aggression as far to the East as possible. Troops have been maintained by several countries in the Federal Republic of Germany in order to maintain this Forward Defense strategy.

THE NATO TRIAD

These developments led to the creation of NATO's own triad of forces to deter possible Soviet/Warsaw Pact aggressive moves into Western Europe. This triad consists of: (1) the U.S. strategic nuclear forces in their three forms including bombers, land-based missiles, and submarine-launched missiles as well as the small British strategic force (bombers as well as missiles in submarines); (2) the U.S. and British theater nuclear forces dedicated to European defense; and (3) the conventional forces of all allied members. Two of the three legs of the triad thus are composed of nuclear forces which produce the major deterrent capability of the alliance. The potential first use of the theater nuclear forces has been considered by NATO to be a critical element which would produce great uncertainly among Soviet leaders if they were to consider seriously any invasion from the East.

The Americans and the British are not alone in providing the nuclear responsibilities for the alliance. Most of the other members share the nuclear burden by having one or more responsibilities regarding deployment of nuclear weapons of various types, such as short-range artillery shells, nuclear depth charges for countries with anti-submarine responsibilities, and longer-range missiles. The Federal Republic of Germany, for example, not only has American and British nuclear weapons stationed on its soil but also has forces of its own which are nuclear capable under a dual-control system.

MODERNIZATION OF NATO'S NUCLEAR FORCES

Modernization of theater nuclear forces has taken place in stages. In 1963, for example, the United States assigned three Polaris submarines to SACEUR to replace IRBMs in Italy and Turkey, and the British assigned its V-bomber force to NATO. The earlier agreement at Nassau in 1962 under which the United States furnished Polaris missiles to the United Kingdom also meant that this force would be assigned eventually to NATO. The adoption of the doctrine of Flexible Response in 1967 recognized that balanced forces needed to be maintained by the alliance in order to meet any aggression at a level, whether conventional or nuclear, sufficient to defeat the threat.

In the face of continued Soviet development and deployment of new nuclear forces, the NATO ministers realized in the late 1970s that the nuclear forces available to the alliance had to be modernized. The deployment of the SS-20 missiles in particular posed a new threat which was not offset by anything in the NATO arsenal. This led directly to the decision in December 1979 to modernize the theater nuclear leg (Intermediate Nuclear Forces--INF) of the NATO triad by the addition of 572 new U.S. missiles to be stationed in several countries as part of their nuclear responsibilities. This consisted of 108 new Pershing II missiles based in the Federal Republic of Germany with an extended range capable of striking targets in the Soviet Union very quickly, and 464 Tomahawk ground-launched cruise missiles (GLCMs) also capable of striking Soviet targets, although more slowly, and based in the United Kingdom, Belgium, the Netherlands, Italy, and the Federal Republic of Germany.

This decision to modernize the NATO INF force was coupled, however, with a second decision to request the U.S. to pursue arms control negotiations with the Soviet Union in the area of theater nuclear weapons. This was the "Dual Track" decision to link deployment of new missiles with the outcome of arms control efforts to reduce the new Soviet SS-20s which now threatened Europe. Although other aspects of allied nuclear deployments had long created problems for arms control efforts between the two superpowers, the INF modernization decision had a special impact.

In the case of the Pershing II missiles, the short flight time to the Soviet Union posed a special problem in the response time for the Soviets. Cruise missiles, too, posed the problem of whether the warheads were nuclear or conventional since both look the same from the outside. Cruise missiles would take longer to reach their targets since they are subsonic, air-breathing missiles, but they would be accurate and very dangerous if launched in large numbers.

Preliminary INF negotiations took place in 1980 and 1981. President Reagan decided to adopt a West German Social Democratic idea when he proposed the

so-called "Zero-Zero Option" in a November 1981 speech
in an attempt to move negotiations forward. This
option was the proposal not to deploy the new U.S.
Pershings and GLCMs in exchange for a Soviet removal of
SS-20s and other missiles deployed in Eastern Europe.
The Soviet Union was not interested in this idea, and
continued to deploy new missiles. The U.S. and NATO
response was to begin deployment of the Pershing II and
Tomahawk cruise missiles late in 1983. This led to a
suspension of all arms control negotiations of any
kind between the United States and Soviet Union by the
end of 1983.

FORWARD-BASED SYSTEMS

     The continued dependence of NATO on nuclear
weapons for a deterrent against possible attack,
although complicating the arms control efforts of the
United States in its negotiations with the Soviet
Union, has been welcomed in Europe because several
countries have seen these weapons as a substitute for
their own defense efforts. They can have more security
for less money. However, well before the 1979 Two
Track decision, nuclear weapons systems in Europe posed
a problem in the Strategic Arms Limitations Talks
(SALT) bargaining process. One of the main problems
concerned the definition of what constitutes strategic
nuclear weapons. From the standpoint of the Soviet
Union, any weapons system which could strike their
country has been considered to be a strategic weapon.
Indeed, this has been one of the main problems
regarding the INF negotiations as well. The United
States has refused to acknowledge that all
Forward-Based Systems (FBS) were strategic in nature.
     This problem had developed early in the SALT I
negotiations. The Soviet Union insisted that Forward-
Based Systems were strategic weapons. Airplanes on
aircraft carriers in the Mediterranean Sea or off the
coast of Europe as well as Air Force planes in Germany
or elsewhere should be counted in the strategic balance
for bargaining purposes if they were nuclear capable
and had the range to strike the Soviet Union. This was
an argument which surprised the United States since it
considered these planes as tactical only and refused to
count them in any strategic balance. The weapons
involved included F-4s and F-111s in Europe and the
United Kingdom and A-4s, A-6s and A-7s on aircraft
carriers. Approximately 600 to 1,000 planes were
involved. The SALT I talks resulted in a trade: the
Soviet Union dropped its insistence regarding FBS, and
the U.S. allowed the USSR to keep its heavy missiles.
Also, some of the differences in the Interim Agreement
ceiling reflected considerations which included FBS.
     In the negotiations after the SALT I agreements,
the Soviet Union again raised the question of obtaining
higher levels of weapons in order to compensate both

for FBS and for other nuclear forces. Although FBS
forces of the United States were considered as
strategic by the Soviet Union, it failed to consider
some of its own weapons systems (Backfire bombers,
other medium-range bombers, and medium- and
intermediate-range missiles) to be strategic since,
although they could strike European targets, they could
not strike the United States. The Vladivostok
Agreement in November 1974 again resulted in an
informal agreement to omit FBS from the negotiations in
exchange for leaving the Soviet heavy ICBMs alone.
There was some concern expressed by the Soviets
afterwards, but the SALT II treaty did not cover FBS.
The assumption was that the "gray area" systems such as
FBS, cruise missiles, SS-20s, and the Backfire bomber
would be covered by SALT III.

THE INDEPENDENT NUCLEAR FORCES

        Another major European complication regarding the
arms control process has been the independent nuclear
forces of both the United Kingdom and France. From the
Soviet perspective, it must face not only the U.S.
weapons but also those of our two European allies and
those of China. Soviet negotiators attempted to
convince the United States that British and French
strategic forces should be included in the Western
count for SALT purposes, but the United Kingdom and
France refused to allow their forces to be counted.
Their argument was that these were independent national
forces not under the control of the United States. No
formal adjustments were made in American ceilings of
weapons to compensate for the allies under the SALT
agreements, but the United States did allow the Soviet
Union a higher number of SLBM launchers in 1972 to
offset concerns about the allies. SALT II failed to
provide any compensation as a result of the Jackson
Amendment which called for strict superpower equality.
        The development of the strategic forces of the two
U.S. allies has not, in the past, posed a great problem
for the arms control process. The original forces were
not so large that they constituted a major threat to
the Soviet Union. Both countries, however, have
engaged in an extensive modernization and expansion
program. The British have decided to build four new
SSBNs which will be fitted with the U.S. built Trident
missile with eight British made MIRVs. This will
provide a major increase in target coverage for the
British. The French, too, have been engaged in a major
program which will modernize their forces. A sixth
SSBN was added recently with a new MIRVed missile
system. Plans call for retrofitting the four newest
Redoutables with the new missile system and replacing
the oldest SSBN with a new design and a new missile.
        The effect of this expansion will be to increase
the percentage of British and French strategic weapons

within the total strategic force of the Western
alliance, especially if the U.S. reduces its force by
withdrawing its 1960s-vintage SSBNs and relies only on
the Ohio-class boats. This increase concerns the
Soviet Union and has resulted in a number of proposals,
including one for direct negotiations between Moscow
and the two European countries. The Soviet Union has,
at different times, considered these forces to be
strategic or intermediate in nature. During the INF
negotiations prior to U.S. deployment, the Soviet
position was that they were intermediate-range weapons,
but since the U.S. has deployed its INF weapons, the
Soviet Union again considers them to be strategic.

Arms control efforts in Europe have also produced
other attempts to reduce nuclear weapons in the area.
For example, at one point in the Mutual and Balanced
Force Reduction Talks in Vienna, a proposal was made to
reduce U.S. battlefield nuclear warheads by 1,000 in
exchange for a reduction in Soviet conventional forces.
Although this proposal was never accepted, it does
illustrate the role which American nuclear weapons in
Europe have in other arms control negotiations.

THE FUTURE OF ARMS CONTROL

Current arms control efforts between the
superpowers resumed in March 1985 when "new
negotiations" began in Geneva. This new set of
negotiations includes the three areas of strategic,
intermediate-range, and space weapons. It takes the
place of the old START and INF talks which had been
ended in late 1983 by the Soviet withdrawal from all
arms control talks. Although much of the attention has
been directed at Soviet attempts to prevent the
development of the U.S. Strategic Defense Initiative
(SDI), negotiations in other areas have progressed to
the point where an agreement on INF weapons could be
concluded separately if the Soviet Union would allow it
to be decoupled from the others.

What options are open to NATO regarding nuclear
weapons and arms control efforts? Numerous
alternatives have been offered as means to escape the
necessity of relying on the potential "first use" of
nuclear weapons as both a deterrent and a part of the
defense of the West.

First, much consideration has been given recently
to the idea of "no first use" of nuclear weapons by
NATO, or, at least, no early first use. The Soviet
Union has accepted this principle in its propaganda,
and it has urged NATO to adopt it, too. NATO has
refused since it depends so heavily on the potential
battlefield use of tactical nuclear weapons to offset
the conventional advantage enjoyed by the Warsaw Pact.
Still, if NATO could increase significantly its
conventional forces in order to present a credible

defense, not only could it adopt a no first use position but possibly a "no use" position as well.

Proposals for increased conventional capabilities of the NATO allies have been widespread. General Bernard Rogers, Supreme Allied Commander Europe, and various study groups have all argued for enhanced conventional forces precisely to present a defense without the need to cross the nuclear threshold. They argue that the only alternative to reliance on strategic and theater nuclear weapons is a more effective conventional force. Fortunately, much of the new technology and many of the new weapons systems adopted by the U.S. Army and Air Force act as major force multipliers in the defense. Although the NATO ministers adopted a 3 percent real increase in defense spending in 1979 in order to build up conventional forces, political pressures have prevented most European members from following this guide. Without a significant increase in conventional weapons, NATO has no choice but to continue its present strategy.

Other options and proposals which have arms control implications include such areas as modifications in the NATO strategy even without an allied conventional build-up. The alliance could rethink its entire defense and its requirements. This might also lead to a decreased emphasis on nuclear weapons as an integral part of the European defense. Redeployment of theater nuclear weapons to areas further in the rear might result in the less likely use of them, especially if conventional forces are effective in the defense. We could also withdraw from Europe a large number of older and outdated nuclear weapons which are no longer part of our current strategy. The AirLand Battle strategy stresses maneuver more than a static defense, and atomic demolition munitions are therefore less critical.

The future remains uncertain regarding nuclear weapons and arms control efforts in Europe. Under present conditions, NATO seems to have no choice but to continue its reliance on nuclear weapons, but a major enhanced conventional defense through new weapons and new tactics and strategies could allow NATO to adopt a "no first use" promise. This is not likely any time soon. In the meantime, NATO's nuclear weapons, combined with the strategic and theater nuclear weapons of both the British and the French, continue to influence and complicate the arms control efforts of the superpowers as they attempt to create a less dangerous world for the future.

REFERENCES

Boutwell, Jeffrey D.; Doty, Paul; and Treverton, Gregory F., eds. The Nuclear Confrontation in Europe. Dover, Mass.: Auburn House Publishing Co., 1985.

Burrows, Bernard, and Edwards, Geoffrey. The Defence
    of Western Europe. London: Butterworth
    Scientific, 1982.

Coffey, Joseph I. Arms Control and European Security.
    New York: Praeger Publishers for the
    International Institute for Strategic Studies,
    1977.

Fedder, Edwin H., ed. Defense Politics of the
    Atlantic Alliance. New York: Praeger Publishers
    1980.

Hagen, Lawrence S., ed. The Crisis in Western
    Security. New York: St. Martin's Press, 1982.

Holm, Hans-Henrik, and Petersen, Nikolaj, eds. The
    European Missiles Crisis: Nuclear Weapons and
    Security Policy. New York: St. Martin's Press,
    1983.

Mearsheimer, John J. "Nuclear Weapons and Deterrence
    in Europe." International Security 9 (Winter
    1984/85): 19-46.

Myers, Kenneth A., ed. NATO: The Next Thirty Years.
    Boulder, Colo.: Westview Press, 1980.

Newhouse, John. Cold Dawn: The Story of SALT. New
    York: Holt, Rinehart & Winston, 1973.

The North Atlantic Treaty Organization: Facts and
    Figures. Brussels: NATO Information Service,
    1981.

Pfaltzgraff, Robert L. Jr., ed. Contrasting
    Approaches to Strategic Arms Control. Lexington,
    Mass.: Lexington Books, 1974.

Schwartz, David N. NATO's Nuclear Dilemmas.
    Washington, D.C.: The Brookings Institution, 1983.

Sigal, Leon V. Nuclear Forces in Europe: Enduring
    Dilemmas, Present Prospects. Washington, D.C.:
    The Brookings Institution, 1984.

Smith, Gerard. Doubletalk: The Story of the First
    Strategic Arms Limitations Talks. Garden City,
    N.Y.: Doubleday & Company, Inc., 1980.

Talbott, Strobe. Endgame: The Inside Story of SALT
    II. New York: Harper & Row, Publishers, 1979.

_____. Deadly Gambits: The Reagan Administration
    and the Stalemate in Nuclear Arms Control. New
    York: Alfred A. Knopf, 1984.

Vigeveno, Guido. The Bomb and European Security.
    Bloomington: Indiana University Press, 1983.

Wolfe, Thomas W. The SALT Experience. Cambridge,
    Mass.: Ballinger Publishing Company, 1979.

8

The Nuclear Pentalogue

Jack R. Perry

When thinking of the perplexing world of nuclear
weapons, we Americans all too often have in mind a
simple dialogue between ourselves and the Soviet Union.
We tend to ignore the nuclear capacities of Great
Britain, France, and China, to belittle the role of
nuclear-capable states like India and others close
behind her, and to assume that nuclear proliferation
will not occur. We prefer to imagine that important
allies of both the United States and the Soviet Union,
countries which have renounced nuclear weapons, do not
have a vital interest or a voice in their dispensation.
We succeed in closing our ears to the voices of other
countries, other peoples.
     In reality, the politics of nuclear weapons is
several-sided. Rather than a nuclear dialogue, we are
in a "nuclear pentalogue," if I may be permitted the
expression: a five-sided dialogue about the critical
nuclear dilemma. The five participants are, first and
second, the United States and the Soviet Union; third,
the American allies in Western Europe and Japan;
fourth, the Soviet allies in Eastern Europe; and fifth,
the rest of the world. My contention is that the
"other" participants in this multivoiced conversation
have important positions and interests which affect the
central nuclear challenge and which make a lessening of
the nuclear danger more complex than we like to admit.
Let us consider in turn the positions of each of the
five great actors in the nuclear drama.

THE UNITED STATES

     If oversimplification is allowed, a popularly
accepted American view of its place in the nuclear era
might be put thus:

>   We developed the A-bomb because of the Nazi
>   danger and we used it on Japan to end the war.
>   We offered to put atomic weapons under inter-
>   national control but the Soviets refused. We

developed the H-bomb for security reasons
against the USSR. For the same reasons, we
developed a succession of technological innovations such as nuclear-missile submarines,
MIRVs, advanced cruise missiles, and so on. We
now propose to develop a nuclear defense for
the same reason, to defend against the Soviet
threat. Because of geography and the preponderance of Soviet conventional military
strength, for our allies' sake we have had to
adopt a policy of using nuclear weapons first,
if we need to. We have tried earnestly to
negotiate arms control measures with the USSR,
but they have cheated a great deal and have
used arms talks as a cover to expand their
arsenals. We have encouraged other countries
not to acquire nuclear weapons, since that
would make a dangerous world; we are willing,
after all, to provide our allies with a nuclear
umbrella. Nuclear weapons may be dangerous, but
they are necessary for our security and that of
the free world, and after all none have been
fired in anger since 1945.

That is indeed an oversimplification, but I submit that
the essence of that view is shared by many Americans,
including some in extremely high places. It is a view
not receptive to the views of other participants in the
pentalogue. In fact, in this view the security of the
United States becomes and almost absolute desideratum,
with some security for our allies as a happy footnote.
     Construction of such a popular oversimplification
for the Soviet Union is a different exercise, because
public opinion plays so small a role in Soviet foreign
policy decisions. Stating a stereotypical view for the
Soviet Politburo is possible, and more to the point.
It would be at a higher level of sophistication,
perhaps, than the American version above; but the
self-justifying nature of the stereotype would be in
close parallel. The Politburo view would see Soviet
nuclear arms as responses to American threats and
initiatives, and would posit a continuing game of
Russian catch-up. And Soviet deafness to other voices
in the nuclear discussion is even more pronounced than
American.
     What is the heart of the American voice in the
nuclear pentalogue? I should suggest it is a search
for security, combined with an awareness for
responsibility to allies, adding in a lingering belief
that the nuclear balance matters politically in the
global U.S.-Soviet rivalry. The overall American
nuclear posture cannot be examined without counting all
three: security, allies, global rivalry.
     If the United States did not take the defense of
its allies so seriously, negotiations with Moscow about
some aspects of the nuclear confrontation would have
gone much more easily. (Then Secretary of State Dean

Rusk said to the NATO Ministerial meeting on December
13, 1967: "Europe is the issue. . . . The Soviet Union
and the United States are not going to fight each other
about polar bears in the Arctic. If Europe were safe,
we and the Soviet Union would have very little to fight
about.") The doctring of first use, the dilemma of
forward-based systems, the intermediate-range missiles
in Europe, and other prickly issues--these stem from
the American geographical position of being separated
by oceans from allies it is pledged to defend.
Similarly, if American decisionmakers truly accepted
the proposition that nuclear weapons have no function
except to deter other nuclear weapons, many of the
worrisome decisions about weapons systems could have
been avoided. Deterrence did not require MIRVs, or
cruise missiles, or the MX missile, or the B-1 bomber;
the political impetus to maintain the appearance of
equality with the Soviet Union--and the will to
maintain that equality--did require them (in the
majority view).
     Moreover, while I have used the term "equality,"
all along there has been a strong undercurrent of
American opinion (which has a counterpart in the USSR)
that nuclear superiority is the only safe goal. The
quest for new technology and new weapons systems may
not have an avowed goal of superiority, but that goal
is implicit in it (on both sides). When both
Washington and Moscow talk about the other side's
threats of "acquiring first-strike capability," this
fear of the political consequences of appearing
inferior is at the bottom of it, more than a real fear
of a real first strike. The debate about the so-called
Strategic Defense Initiative (SDI)--more correctly the
renewed debate about the advantages and the
destabilizing disadvantages of nuclear
defenses--ultimately stems from that political fear of
appearing inferior as much as from the real fear of
becoming militarily vulnerable.
     Having drawn up a definition of "security" that is
tied to a multiform nuclear arsenal accepted as equal
or superior to the Soviet arsenal, American
policymakers are not prepared to accept "being number
two." They must be prepared to reason on the level of
the stereotype given above. They are prepared to
accept the dangers of the "first-use doctrine," the
danger of nuclear war through accident or escalation,
even some danger of the militarization of American
society, but not nuclear inferiority.
     Americans like to make much of the Soviet record
of not living up to treaties on arms control, but do
not like to recognize their own failings in this
regard, such as the pledge in the preamble to the
Non-Proliferation Treaty of 1968 to "achieve at the
earliest possible date the cessation of the nuclear
arms race and to undertake effective measures in the
direction of nuclear disarmament." That is the law of
the land. The Soviets interpret this pledge in the

same way as we Americans do, but other countries look at it more seriously.

The operational U.S. government assumption is that the non-nuclear countries will agree to remain non-nuclear, as if the political "inferiority" their non-nuclear status implied did not matter. Similarly, U.S. policymakers tend to assume that our allies will continue to view their security as a lesser part of American security. But this assumption too may be unravelling. Finally, American policymakers do not waste worry on the security concerns of the rest of the world beyond NATO and the Warsaw Pact; but that voice may yet be heard from.

It is often argued that in the search for security, the United States has wound up being less secure, in the profound sense of protecting its continued existence, than it ever was between 1776 and 1945. American leaders are aware of this fact philosophically, but not operationally; it does not enter into nuclear weapons decisions. Given "the other nuclear triad" to which I have been alluding--nuclear weapons as security, as protection for allies, and as political counters in the global rivalry--the United States seems wedded to its reliance on its nuclear arsenal. Only a decided shift in public opinion, possibly combined with the raising of other voices in the nuclear pentalogue, could cause a change.

THE SOVIET UNION

Equating the two superpowers as political actors is common in writings about arms control, but it is unrealistic. The two giants arrive at policies and decisions in astoundingly different ways, and this affects their political discourse. The United States suffers from the faults of a huge, diverse, unruly democracy; its policy paths are meandering and its changes abrupt. The Soviet Union suffers from the faults of a huge, diverse, dictatorial empire; its policy paths are secret and removed from easy analysis. "Security," "allies," and many other words mean quite different things to American and Soviet policymakers.

Public opinion exists in the Soviet Union, but it plays quite a different role than it does in the United States. In the USSR, it would more correctly be labeled "public acceptance or resistance," and it affects foreign policy relatively little in normal times. The Soviet Politburo rules, it is always good to remind ourselves, without the consent of the governed, and with the indispensable support of the secret police. Politburo members pay close attention, I assume, to KGB reports of popular acceptance of, or resistance to, economic directions and directives; but they are not accustomed to worrying about the foreign policy views of ordinary Russians, and much less of Estonians or Uzbeks. In the non-Soviet parts of the

Soviet empire, in particular in Eastern Europe,
independence fades when it comes to foreign policy, and
it vanishes when it comes to nuclear matters. The
Soviet leaders do not trust their Warsaw Pact allies,
and in the matter of nuclear weapons the iron
preoccupations with Soviet security take over.

The Soviet vision of security encompasses first of
all the safety of the Communist regime, and then the
Soviet homeland, with Eastern Europe and other
borderland areas (Mongolia and, alas, now Afghanistan)
as part of a protective glacis. The Soviet leaders
have a strong belief in what they see as the Soviet
mission in the world--incorporating a lofty assessment
of Russia's history as a Great Power--but they combine
this belief with strong feelings of insecurity and
inferiority. In the nuclear dialogue, these
semi-paranoiac feelings center on American intentions
and unpredictability, together with an awe for Western
technological prowess. Starting from what Stalin must
have felt was a severe position of inferiority in 1945,
the Soviet leaders have seldom wavered in passionately
seeking nuclear parity, if not a degree of superiority,
with the United States. And because of Russian
traditions and Soviet technology, they have sought
Soviet security in large numbers of weapons, huge
weapon sizes, and generally in what American would
consider overdoing it. It if is catch-up, the American
might say, it is catch-up gone mad.

The Soviet system incorporates propaganda into its
policymaking, something the United States has not
learned to do except in an occasional amateurish way.
Appealing to "world public opinion"--especially to West
European and at times to American opinion--is a part of
the Soviet approach to nuclear issues. To buttress
their appeal, the Soviet leaders are willing to make
some occasional concessions in their negotiating
positions. But except for propaganda, the Soviet
leaders can be surprisingly ruthless in disregarding
the views of the rest of the world--including of course
their long-suffering allies--in their nuclear policy
calculations. They are sublime realists, first and
foremost, and security is the most real thing they
know. (It has been remarked that "security" is a much
stronger word in Russian than in English. The Latin
root of our word means "without care," whereas the
Russian word bezopasnost' means literally "without
danger.")

The Soviet voice in the pentalogue is that of
ruthless men who are largely free of concern about
public opinion. (Only the United States has used
nuclear weapons, but only the Soviet Union, in the
person of Khrushchev, has to my knowledge publicly
threatened the use of them.) What the Soviet leaders
might do with nuclear weapons if they had a free hand
is a matter for painful conjecture, but they are keenly
aware that their hands are not free; they show acute
sensitivity to the possibility of American use of

nuclear arms. They see American leaders as unreliable, changeable, aggressive, trigger-happy. They worry about our first-use doctrine, and fear that escalation in a regional conflict could lead to all-out exchange and to the destruction of the Bolshevik regime in Russia. Despite the ritual propaganda slogans about the eventual triumph of communism even in case of a nuclear war, all the evidence shows that the Soviet leaders actually have deep fear of a nuclear conflict, and wonder if their regime might survive it.

Against this background, it is clear that the Soviet Union will continue to be exceedingly cautious in any nuclear negotiations. Their voice in the nuclear pentalogue is attuned above all to the American threat. Seeing American technology as threatening, and viewing their political predominance in Europe as essential to their security, the Soviet leaders are not about to bargain away any positions of strength. Yet they apparently are not blind to the danger of more insecurity arising within their quest for security.

WESTERN EUROPE AND JAPAN

No country enjoys having to depend for its security on another country: perhaps that is a good starting point for thinking about the third voice in the nuclear pentalogue, the West Europeans and the Japanese. After the shocks of World War II and the advent of the Cold War, with the United States looming super-large on the world scene and the Soviet Union seen as a danger, it was not unnatural for the peoples of Western Europe and Japan to throw themselves gladly under the American nuclear umbrella.

Power relationships have changed mightily since then. The great current question is the extent to which America's allies at both sides of the Eurasian land mass are growing apart from the United States in popular attitudes--and thus eventually in governmental attitudes, since these are democratic countries-- towards the nuclear rivalry and the U.S.-Soviet relationship. Is a long-term drawing apart in progress?

The backdrop to this process is the evolution in European and Asian views of the United States after the assassination of President Kennedy and the long Vietnam drama. America came to be less a shining knight than simply another Great Power, with all the old Great Power habits. The fact that the Soviet Union was seen far more negatively still did not alter the decline in American prestige. A different perception of "the Soviet threat"--always seen more in military terms in America than in Europe--led to differing views of defense needs. For a time, a strong anti-nuclear movement seemed to eat at the foundation of the American-West European relationship. This influence has abated, although concern about nuclear weapons will

probably continue to erode popular support for some
American military policies. Some observers do see the
growth of a European attitude that says: "What's in
the nuclear competition for us?" The great advantages
may be perceived increasingly as going to the two
superpowers, leaving the others with certain risks
which might be balanced carefully against certain
security gains. (Obviously attitudes vary, and the
foregoing is a generalization of generalizations. NATO
Allies, Japan, and South Korea will have different
policies from the neutrals, and from each other, and
the two great defeated powers of World War II have
special positions. Of course the two West European
nuclear weapon states, France and Great Britain, have
particular roles.)

The need for reliance on the American nuclear
umbrella is still felt strongly by the governments and
the political elites of Western Europe and Japan.
Doubts about the American commitment--the willingness
to use the nuclear weapon in defense of its allies--are
always present; possibly the Strategic Defense
Initiative (SDI), with its echoes of Fortress America,
will increase those fears. Certainly Europeans will
wish to be involved in "Star Wars" research--a European
Minister told Martin Hillenbrand of the University of
Georgia that Europe could not resist taking part in
"the biggest pork barrel in history." But the fears of
"decoupling," or more broadly of a lessening of the
American attachment to the defense of Europe, may grow
along with SDI spending.

The U.S. record of consultations with its European
allies about strategic arms limitation talks has been
good, all things considered. Yet the major tides in
American arms control policy are not "consultable" in
American usage--the decision not to press for
ratification of SALT II, the virtual withdrawal of the
Reagan Administration from the arms control process in
1981, the announcement of SDI in 1983. American allies
with some justification see their vital security needs
being treated as minor footnotes to American political
decisions. As they often remind us, they do not get to
vote for the American President.

Great Britain and France have plans to upgrade
their nuclear forces considerably. Although those
plans could become subject to the strategic arms
discussions, the United States has generally applauded
them and offered its help. Possibly because of an
American lens that sees conflicts and political
tensions almost wholly in terms of the U.S.-Soviet
relationship, the United States treats French and
British nuclear upgrading as a help to Western
security, tending to ignore the problems that this
could eventually cause with the nations which have
pledged to remain non-nuclear, such as the Federal
Republic of Germany and Italy. Are they to remain in a
perpetually "inferior" position? If serious efforts to
reduce nuclear weaponry are absent, may not the

division of the world into nuclear "haves" and
"have-nots" become more productive of friction?

This third great force in the nuclear pentalogue
seems to be arguing for a scaling down of the nuclear
danger through negotiations. It still mistrusts the
Soviet Union, still relies on the United States for
security, but is less comfortable than it used to be
with the direction the nuclear rivalry is going. This
voice may get louder.

EASTERN EUROPE

Except for Yugoslavia, the Communist-ruled
countries of Eastern Europe are uneasily part of the
Soviet sphere of interest. Theirs is an unnatural
situation. The peoples are all Western, and if it were
not for the tragedy of Stalin's absorption of their
countries into his empire in 1945 and after, they would
by now be well-integrated parts of the American-
European community of the North Atlantic. The leaders
are all nominally Communist, but the differences among
a Jaruselski, a Kadar, a Zhivkov, a Husak, a Ceausescu,
or a Honecker are probably greater than their
similarities. Although they are dependent upon Moscow,
all of these leaders want more independence. Nearly
all of their subject populations despise the Soviets,
and would like as much distance as possible from Soviet
domination. Even the military are dependable only up
to a point. The Soviets do not trust any of them--the
secret police first, the leaders second, the military
third, and the people last would be their order of
"trusting"--and they would never allow Poles or
Hungarians or Czechs or East Germans to get their
fingers on a nuclear trigger.

In the nuclear conundrum, the more than one
hundred million people of Communist-ruled Eastern
Europe therefore are in the most peculiar position of
anybody. Eastern Europe depends for its "security" on
the Soviet Union, and the "threat" is from the United
States and its allies. Yet the populations, and
perhaps the leaders, feel that their countries are, in
the main, a potential battleground between the two
superpowers. They know that their security interests
weigh very lightly as compared with the leaden weight
of Soviet interests, and they certainly know that
Moscow does not listen to them in making nuclear
policy. East Europeans wish that the old ideas of
nuclear-free zones in Central Europe and the Balkans
were somehow realizable; but they know that this is
unlikely. Meanwhile, the placement of American
intermediate-range missiles has brought all of Eastern
Europe for the first time within the range of theater
nuclear weapons.

When I was serving as Ambassador to Bulgaria in
1979-81, and the U.S. development of Pershing II and
cruise missiles in Europe was being debated, the

Bulgarians made heated use of the argument that for the
first time, missiles in Europe could reach their soil
and would be aimed at them. I was not sure what the
immense difference was between ICBMs aimed at them from
Germany and ICBMs aimed at them from farther away, but
it seemed to make a considerable psychological
difference to them.

The voice of the East European participant in the
nuclear pentalogue is a very faint voice, hardly
listened to in the West, hardly listened to anymore in
Moscow. The East Europeans know that their leverage
with Moscow is limited. The Soviets see any
fundamental change in Eastern Europe as undermining
their vital security interests, as 1956 and 1968
showed: they are determined that Eastern Europe will
be part of the Soviet security system, even if internal
loosening up takes place within bounds. East European
dependence on Moscow economically as well as
politically lessens the chances of any very strong
participation by the East Europeans in the nuclear
debate. So "pressure" from Eastern Europe on Moscow is
modest, but it does exist.

Within the framework of the Warsaw Pact, somewhat
less so in COMECON, what the East Europeans say does
carry some weight. The satisfactory functioning of
their economies and of their military establishments,
as well as the keeping of internal order, does matter
to the Kremlin. And any possibility of unrest or
popular alienation because of security
concerns--concerns growing out of the nuclear
pentalogue--of course affects the Soviets.

At the beginning of the Reagan Administration, the
perception of President Reagan as a "nuclear cowboy"
helped the Soviets for a time. But as talks got
underway, and as the SS-20 missiles were announced for
stationing in Eastern Europe, strong undercurrents
began to rise to the surface. The feeble-but-still-
existing public opinion in the East European countries
brought modest pressure to bear on the leaders; and the
leaders, insecure as they are, brought modest pressure
on Moscow to work at reducing the nuclear danger. This
amounts to very little in the grand scale of influences
in the nuclear arms race, but it is there.

THE REST OF THE WORLD

It would be comforting, in a way, to write that
the fifth voice in the nuclear pentalogue is the voice
of a united mankind crying out for nuclear sanity.
That is not the case. The "voice of the rest of the
world" is not a unified voice at all. There is China;
there are neutrals like Sweden that could be nuclear
powers if they wished; there are Muslim countries who
believe acquisition of nuclear weapons would help
redress the balance of regional power against
adversaries like India or Israel; there are Latin

American countries with ambitions for a larger and more
recognized place in the sun; there are countries like
Japan and Germany which are true Great Powers but which
have genuinely renounced nuclear weapons, at least for
the present generation and probably beyond; there are
many poor countries with no real hope of acquiring
nuclear weapons, ever; and underneath it all, there are
vast millions of people in all countries who stand to
suffer if military costs eat up their subsistence, who
stand to perish if full-scale nuclear war comes.

The Chinese position in the nuclear pentalogue is
singular, for it is the only nuclear-weapon state
against whom each of the other super-powers presumably
has nuclear weapons targeted. It is not a true ally of
either of them. It cherishes its role of leadership
among the developing countries, and makes resistance to
the hegemonial ambitions of both Moscow and Washington
a vociferous part of its foreign policy.

China is something of a wild card, if one may use
the term, in the nuclear debate, since it is not part
of any alliance. In the arms control arena, its
positions have had much the same effect as those of
France, which, although a member of the North Atlantic
Alliance, has since 1966 kept its military policies,
particularly its nuclear ones, a matter of
self-determination. The political weight of the
possession of nuclear weapons is a telling matter for
Beijing, since its deterrent force alone could hardly
maintain its security against the most likely
adversary, the Soviet Union. Being a permanent member
of the Security Council and one of the major
nuclear-weapon states is of great importance,
especially in the light of Chinese cultural and
political history: this is the mark of China's
reemergence upon the world scene as a Great Power.

If there is talk of lowering numbers of nuclear
weapons, therefore, the Chinese would probably take the
stance that the two superpowers are so far ahead that
they should make deep cuts before the other
nuclear-weapon states make serious changes in their
arsenals and plans. France, and possibly even Great
Britain, might take similar approaches. Thus China
does represent an element in the nuclear equation that
has great complicating potential, if ever the dialogue
turns towards reductions that have any meaning in
security terms. Meanwhile China represents a kind of
political pressure on the two superpowers to consider
whether their own "security" justifies such nuclear
predominance that other important states must face
great relative "insecurity" as a result. In nuclear
negotiations now underway, the Chinese look upon
superpower machinations with suspicion, always
concerned that any lessening of the U.S.-Soviet
confrontation might result in more nuclear weapons
pointed at China, especially from Soviet soil. China
plays a particular role in the nuclear pentalogue by
reminding other actors that the vital security

interests of some countries are at stake in decisions that are marginal in security terms for the main actors.

In the light of the diversity of "the rest of the world," clearly it would be foolish for any writer on these perplexing subjects to say that if one only listened to "the voice of humanity," nuclear disarmament would come and peace would reign. People want all sorts of things, and follow all sorts of leaders; peace is not usually at the top of their list of desiderata, and disarmament is not usually on the popular agenda at all. The United States is probably as democratic in the formulation of its foreign policy as any major state, and Americans would hardly consider themselves warmongers. Yet they approved the use of the atomic bomb against Japan; they generally have approved the development of the vast nuclear arsenal; and they have consistently favored "policies of strength" when it came to defense budgets and military balances. "Bomber gaps," "missile gaps," and "windows of vulnerability," all proved fictional after elections, have all helped win elections, and no candidate for President has won since World War II on a platform of lowering the level of the military balance with the Soviet Union.

The deathblow to ratification of SALT II may have been the Soviet invasion of Afghanistan at Christmas in 1979, but the tide had been turning against SALT in public opinion for some time before; and in the pivotal year of 1978, when completion and ratification of SALT II might have been possible, the American people and key congressional leaders did not come to its support. (See General Seignious' chapter in this volume.) In public opinion, as in the councils of government, nuclear arms control continuously takes a back seat to other goals.

Yet as the nuclear arms race between Washington and Moscow continues to run, with escalation into vaster numbers of warheads, into new and more staggering combinations of weapons systems, whether labeled offensive or defensive, into new regions of danger for a descent into nuclear war that could end human life on our planet, it does appear that both governments and peoples in the non-nuclear-weapon countries are becoming more impatient with the present condition. Increasingly, statesmen and ordinary people are saying that their security is being sacrificed to American and Russian conceptions of their security--and possibly false conceptions, at that. "Why," they seem to be saying, "should the superpowers decide the shape of my future?"

One danger this protest is directed against, if I read it correctly, is that of nuclear proliferation. (See the chapter by Brito and Intriligator in this volume.) Many governments are itching to get the nuclear bomb, for all kinds of reasons. If the nuclear powers do not take seriously their pledge in the

Non-Proliferation Treaty to reduce the level of weapons and to seek nuclear disarmament, why should the states who denied themselves nuclear weapons continue to live by _their_ pledge? The facile answer we give them is that everyone's security is involved, for if one country in a region gets the bomb, surely its neighbors will follow suit, and proliferation will result in less security for everyone. This is good logic, but why should Pakistan or Israel or Iraq or Argentina follow this logic if the United States and the Soviet Union do not? If present nuclear-weapon states find nuclear weapons useful enough that they refuse to shed them, even at the cost of lessened real security for all, then why should the current non-nuclear states not follow their example? And if proliferation should begin in earnest--it is there, latent, and one or two public announcements of "going nuclear" could trigger the race--where would it stop? Could one expect Germany and Japan to continue their self-denial policy forever? And would the world not turn far more dangerous very fast?

The fifth voice in the nuclear pentalogue, diverse as it is, seems to ask a central question about the existence of nuclear weapons, especially at their current high levels: "Whose security, if anybody's is being increased?" Public opinion in the democratic countries focuses on wasted money, on skewed priorities, on the perils of nuclear winter. Governments talk about the diversion of technology into space weapons rather than earthly development, and about the sacrifice of their security for the dubious conceptions of security clung to by the nuclear powers. The direction of both public opinion and governments is the same. The rest of the world casts doubts on the sanity and utility of the present nuclear situation. It presses for some change towards a less perilous world.

This fifth voice speaks, of course, for different purposes, arguing for different paths. The Greens in West Germany, Khaddafi or Khomeini, Botha of South Africa, Lutheran demonstrators in East Germany, SANE in the United States, the Swedes and Swiss and Austrians--it would be impossible to rally them behind any one approach to the nuclear dilemma. And the United Nations, which faithfully represents this enormous variety, is, alas, probably powerless to pull itself together to find any new, unified path to nuclear solutions. There is, most of us would agree, great need for world accord--and little chance of it.

Still, the recognition of the challenge is the necessary beginning of coping with it. Rethinking is the starting point. We Americans have fallen into the habit of thinking that our legitimate security needs interact with Soviet security concerns, that we two have every right to determine the nuclear future. That is a dangerous assumption. It leaves out the variety of voices which make progress towards nuclear solutions

more difficult than we imagine, squinting through our
bipolar lens. And it leaves out the dangers of a
proliferated world, if the two superpowers ignore the
other voices. I would argue, therefore, that to move
from the concept of a nuclear dialogue to that of a
nuclear pentalogue is the beginning of wisdom in
nuclear discourse.

PART 3

Nuclear Deterrence and American National Interest

9

Options for U.S. National Security Policy

Mark Garrison

The Center for Foreign Policy Development at Brown
University and the Public Agenda Foundation have for
many years studied the role of the public in affecting
key public policy issues. The guiding principle in
this joint undertaking is that any resolution of
troubling national issues, particularly one so crucial
as arms control and nuclear weapons can only come about
through full engagement of the public. This means that
everyone--public, experts, and political leaders--must
focus first on fundamental choices about which all
Americans, whatever their level of expertise, can make
judgments based on sound instincts.

PRIORITIES

The search for choices should begin by focusing on
priorities, asking ourselves not just "what do we
want?" but "what do we want above all else?"
Specifically, Americans should weigh whether our
highest priority is to avoid nuclear war, or whether
there are other goals which would take precedence under
some circumstance.
The only other priority that can compete with
avoiding nuclear war is the goal of protecting major
values Americans consider essential, such as embracing
freedom and all the other concepts and material things
we value for ourselves and others. In order to
simplify the discussion, this can be called "protecting
our interests." The basic question is, Do Americans
believe it more important to avoid a Soviet nuclear
attack on the United States or to protect our other
interests?
One difficulty in thinking about priorities is
getting the right fix on consequences and risks. Some
maintain that we cannot be sure that a nuclear war
would destroy human life on earth, or even the United
States. Others put it the other way around: We cannot
be sure it would not. President Reagan recently put it
succinctly, saying that even a nuclear exchange

intended to take out missile silos could "wipe out the earth as we know it. (Reagan interview, New York _Times_, February 12, 1985).

Let us examine the two choices of priorities a little more closely.

Highest Priority On Avoiding Nuclear War

Those who believe that the avoidance of nuclear war should be our highest national priority, even at the cost of other important objectives, argue that the consequences of a nuclear war would be so disastrous for America, and possibly for all human civilization, that nothing is worth risking that outcome even if the probabilities are very small.

Of course a nuclear war started by someone else cannot be avoided, and at present the only protection from such attack is to deter it by threatening retaliation in kind. Some marginal steps could be taken to reduce the danger of accidental launches, and to avoid backing the Soviets into a desperate, suicidal nuclear attack. But the following argument focuses mainly on avoiding a nuclear war which the U.S. would start.

To take the most extreme and hypothetical case: according to this reasoning, even if the United States itself were about to be overwhelmed by foreign soldiers, it would make no sense to initiate a mutually suicidal nuclear war. An occupying army could be fought in the hills, sabotaged, undermined, and eventually hounded out of the country. So long as Americans lived who were willing to sacrifice themselves personally for the sake of the American idea, there would be hope. Mass suicide would be no solution, even if it took the enemy to oblivion as well.

According to this argument, if it makes no sense to be willing to commit societal suicide to repel a hypothetical invasion of the United States, it makes even less sense to do so for the sake of lesser causes. Therefore we should be straight in our own minds that nothing takes precedence over avoiding nuclear war, even though we have no choice but to threaten nuclear retaliation to deter nuclear attack.

Highest Priority On Protecting Our Interests

The opposite school of thought, not often expressed overtly but nevertheless an important part of many Americans' thinking, takes the view that our most important goal is to make sure that Americans remain free to continue our way of life. We should regard the defense of our closest allies the same as our own defense, reasoning that if we do not help them stop an

aggressor we will eventually have to fight that
aggressor by ourselves.

This reasoning lies behind the long-established
policy of extending the protection of our nuclear
arsenal also to our allies, in particular the NATO
countries in Europe, as well as Japan and South Korea.
Our policy is not only to threaten nuclear retaliation
for a nuclear attack on our allies, but also to
threaten to initiate the use of nuclear weapons if
necessary to stop non-nuclear aggression if it is about
to overwhelm them.

The argument for putting highest priority on
protecting our interests rather than on avoiding
nuclear war thus boils down to this: we should do
everything we can to avoid nuclear war, but when the
chips are down we should take our chances in a nuclear
war rather than risk the possible loss of those things
that matter most to us as a people.

Those who favor putting top priority on protecting
our interests argue that the more clearly we
demonstrate the will to use nuclear weapons, the less
likely it is that we will ever have to use them. This
creates a great temptation to say that we do not have
to choose between American interests and avoiding
nuclear war--we can give them equal priority and
achieve both. It is a persuasive argument for many
Americans. The response of those who disagree is that
we cannot be convincing in our threat to be first to
use nuclear weapons unless we really mean it, and if we
do mean it we are accepting the risk that an opponent's
stupidity or desperation somewhere far from American
soil will take our fate out of our hands.

POLICIES

Americans need to weigh not only the priorities we
assign to ends, but also our choice of means. The
options available for implementing priorities--whether
first priority is placed on avoiding nuclear war or
protecting our other interests--can be considered under
three categories:

1. Nuclear weapons policies--policies for
developing and deploying them, strategies for using
them to carry out our aims, policies on developing and
deploying technical means of defending against nuclear
weapons, and negotiations to control them

2. International policies for advancing American
aims on matters and in places which might constitute
proximate causes of war

3. Policies for dealing with the Soviet Union on
matters which can affect the underlying causes of war

Each of these categories will be discussed and our
options will be considered in the framework of our
overall priorities.

Weapons, Defenses, Negotiations

Nuclear weapons choices are complex and bewildering in part because we try to consider strategy, technical weapons issues, and negotiating tactics all together. It is difficult, if not impossible, to do so in a way that leads to clear-cut public choice. In order to focus on fundamentals, we should ask the question, what purpose do we want nuclear weapons to serve? (Voter Options, 1984). There are four possible answers.

First, the answer can be "none"--nuclear weapons serve no useful purpose and should therefore be mutually abolished by all states that have them as soon as possible. This option assumes that all nuclear powers will go along and will be satisfied with relying on means other than nuclear weapons to protect themselves from traditional types of aggression. The strongest argument for this approach is that civilization cannot afford indefinitely to rely on a "balance of terror," a threat of mutual suicide, because eventually it will break down and bring about the end of civilization. The strongest argument against it is that mankind will always have the knowledge of how to build nuclear weapons, and a small number of bombs secretly built--or hidden away during mutual disarmament--could give overwhelming power to unscrupulous leaders.

The second answer is that nuclear weapons have only one purpose--to prevent nuclear attack. This option would require only sufficient nuclear forces to make sure no one would dare attack with nuclear weapons; this tends to put a ceiling on the number of weapons needed, since--if the weapons are capable of surviving a first strike--you only need enough to destroy the enemy's society once. It also means that if potential enemies reduce their nuclear arsenals, you can reduce yours, since the only purpose of yours is to make sure theirs are not used. Like the first option, it assumes that we and our allies can be satisfied with non-nuclear forces to defend ourselves from non-nuclear attack. The strongest argument for this option is that by giving up the threat of mutual suicide to defend against non-nuclear attack we would reduce the chances of nuclear war, and could better defend ourselves and our friends with usable, non-nuclear weapons than by threatening nuclear suicide. The strongest argument against this approach is that NATO and the U.S. are most unified and secure if we show we are willing to use nuclear weapons despite the risk to ourselves.

The third answer is that nuclear weapons have two purposes--to prevent anyone from attacking us with nuclear weapons, as in the second option, and also to prevent enemy tanks and soldiers from overrunning our allies even if the enemy does not use nuclear weapons. This option has been U.S. and NATO policy for decades, embodying a threat to be first to use nuclear weapons

if necessary to stop aggression. It requires an
extensive nuclear arsenal so that we can pose a
credible threat at all levels, from battlefield nuclear
weapons right up through intercontinental missiles.
The strongest argument for this option is that it has
kept the peace in Western Europe for nearly 40 years,
and to scrap it now might undermine our alliances. The
strongest argument against it is that existing Soviet
and American nuclear arsenals make any use of nuclear
weapons by either side suicidal for both; any limited
use would escalate to all-out nuclear war.

The fourth answer is that nuclear weapons have
many uses beyond the ones already mentioned:
preventing Soviet expansion in many places, not just
those countries with which we have alliances; competing
successfully with the Soviet Union in the most
unambiguous measure of military power, nuclear weapons;
and effectively backing up our political objectives
throughout the world. Some elements of this option
have also been U.S. policy through the decades, and
still are. This policy would be most effective with
demonstrated US nuclear superiority over potential
enemies, but if that is not possible, then at least the
U.S. should maintain the most extensive
state-of-the-art nuclear arsenal possible. The
strongest argument for this approach is that if our
actions and words clearly demonstrate a willingness and
ability to use nuclear weapons, American interests will
be safer. The strongest argument against it is that
efforts to coerce the Soviet Union with nuclear weapons
will only result in a spiraling arms race and,
eventually, confrontation and war.

Those four options, based on the purpose we
believe nuclear weapons should serve--no purpose,
single purpose, dual purpose and multiple
purpose--provide a useful framework for thinking about
many points currently being debated. The usefulness of
the framework can be illustrated, in this brief
discussion, by focusing on option two, which is based
on the belief that nuclear weapons should serve only
the purpose of protecting us and our allies from
nuclear attack. Recent polls show that three out of
four Americans prefer this approach, even though it
runs counter to what U.S. policy has been for decades.
If you choose this option, you would favor maintaining
a strong nuclear deterrent primarily in the air and
under the seas, since such forces are less vulnerable
to surprise attack and could deliver devastating
retaliation after a nuclear attack. You would likely
be against the MX missile, because it is vulnerable to
a Soviet first strike and would serve no purpose, since
under this option we would not plan a first strike
ourselves. You would probably be willing to negotiate
a freeze on both U.S. and Soviet nuclear weapons at
current levels, on the grounds that we have plenty to
make sure the Soviets never start using them. You
would favor an agreement which reduced nuclear weapons

on both sides, and would be particularly anxious to
negotiate the removal of all short-range weapons from
Europe on both sides, since they would serve no purpose
and are dangerous to keep around. You might be willing
to go along with the Europeans if they want to keep our
intermediate-range nuclear weapons in Europe to assure
against a Soviet nuclear attack on Europe.

      You would favor building up U.S. and NATO
non-nuclear defense capabilities to the extent
necessary to deter non-nuclear aggression.
Furthermore, if someone pointed out to you that the
West Europeans might be panicked if we suddenly
reversed our long-standing policy, you would probably
agree to phase in the new policy gradually, building up
non-nuclear defenses while gradually reducing reliance
on nuclear weapons down to the point where we did not
need to rely on them at all.

      If, on the other hand, you choose the indefinite
pursuit of options three or four--using nuclear weapons
for purposes other than preventing nuclear attack on
the U.S.--you would take a different, more positive
view of new and increasingly effective nuclear weapons.
Since your purposes would be most effectively achieved
by regaining nuclear superiority over the USSR, you
might be tempted to pursue that goal, despite
disappointments in the past when the Soviets managed to
overcome our breakthroughs and in some cases, such as
putting multiple warheads on missiles, to turn them to
their advantage. You would probably feel that the most
promising avenue is to try to use our technological
advantages to achieve new breakthroughs which would
vault us again into the lead. Even if you do not
advocate deliberate pursuit of superiority, you would
be sensitive to even marginal Soviet weapons advances,
and to any negotiating concessions which might now or
in the future cause the Soviets to doubt that the U.S.
would be first to use nuclear weapons if necessary to
protect our interests.

      How do our priorities affect these weapons
options? They may be directly related. If you place
priority on avoiding nuclear war, you are more likely
to favor shifting to options one and two, which forego
the first use of nuclear weapons by the U.S. If you
place highest priority on protecting U.S. interests,
even at the risk of nuclear war, you will favor
continuing to base U.S. policy on three and four, which
threaten first use of nuclear weapons if necessary to
protect U.S. interests.

      Using the four options as a tool for thinking
about the problem leads to useful insights. Even many
of those who strongly advocate nuclear modernization in
the short term also advocate moving to abolish nuclear
weapons entirely in the long term . President Reagan
not only sets the abolition of nuclear weapons as a
goal, but has presented a plan for achieving that goal
by means of building up defenses which, if it worked,
could make it possible for both the U.S. and the Soviet

Union to abolish their offensive nuclear weapons
(Reagan speech, March 23, 1983).

Leaving aside for the moment the feasibility of
achieving effective defenses, and the arguments about
whether the pursuit of such defenses could be
destabilizing and dangerous in the interim period, we
can consider how the President's Strategic Defense
Initiative (SDI) fits into the framework of choices we
are developing. In the first place, his ultimate goal,
the abolition of nuclear weapons, may mean that we put
our highest priority on avoiding nuclear war, since if
we put our highest priority on defending our other
interests, we would reasonably wish to retain nuclear
weapons indefinitely as our defense of last resort. It
means that we are willing to take our chances with
depending on means other than nuclear weapons to defend
our other interests. It also suggests a gradual shift
from our present reliance on options three and four,
through a transition period when we still rely on
nuclear weapons to deter nuclear attack but not to
deter non-nuclear attack, until finally we reach the
stage when either through sophisticated defenses or
sophisticated means of verification and control we are
able to feel secure in eliminating nuclear weapons
altogether.

In some respects, the transition toward options
two and one appears already to have begun. The Reagan
Administration and NATO have embarked on a policy of
developing non-nuclear military capabilities in order
to reduce reliance on nuclear weapons. Neither NATO
nor the American Administration are prepared to talk
about setting a goal of completely eliminating reliance
on nuclear weapons for deterrence of non-nuclear
attack, much less a timetable for getting there. Yet
that goal is implied in the President's long-term goal
of eventually abolishing nuclear weapons altogether, or
rendering them impotent. It may be premature to speak
of a basic shift in American policy on nuclear weapons.
But clearly it is time to begin discussing openly and
frankly these fundamental issues of goals, priorities,
and options.

Regarding the President's proposals on strategic
defense, we may wish to spend money, even a lot of
money, on research to find out what the possibilities
are; we should be clear that the objective is not
unilateral advantage, and we should take whatever
concrete steps are necessary to make that plain,
including ironclad legislative restrictions on going
beyond research into testing and deployment, if that is
what it takes to keep the Soviets from breaking out of
present limitations on offensive systems and to achieve
significant reductions of nuclear weapons on both
sides.

We must of course recognize that fully effective
defense may never be achievable, and that the answers
may not be in before the next century begins. If we
are, meanwhile, investigating other paths toward the

same goal--if we are at least working toward
eliminating any possibility that we Americans will
someday find ourselves with no choice in defending
something that seems important other than deliberately
starting the nuclear war that will end everything--we
could make ourselves and the world a little safer
without a defense against missiles.

International Policies

From weapons policies, let us now turn to the next
category of means for pursuing our objectives,
international policies. If we decided that our highest
priority is to avoid nuclear war rather than to protect
U.S. interests, what effect would that choice have on
American policies for dealing with those areas of the
world and those issues which are so crucial to either
the U.S. or the USSR or both that they could lead to
war?

As discussed previously above, choosing avoidance
of nuclear war as our highest priority would mean a
decision not to initiate the use of nuclear weapons to
defend American interests. But clearly, whatever our
decision about overall priorities, we need to make wise
judgments about what and where our vital interests are.
Whether we intend to defend them by starting a nuclear
war or by shedding young Americans' blood, we should be
certain that the "interest" is truly vital. And even
if we retain the threat of using nuclear weapons as the
fallback means of defending something, we should try
first to handle the problem by other means.

We must also recognize that in some places and
circumstances our country may not be willing to apply
the resources and determination necessary to prevail.
Before allowing ourselves to be boxed into no-win
situations, we should ask ourselves the tough
questions: What do we want to defend? And what
sacrifices are we prepared to make to defend it? Our
entire country, in a nuclear war? Our young people's
lives, in a conventional war? Should we limit our
involvement to giving arms to those who are willing to
fight for their freedom? Should we concentrate on
economic aid, to try and cure one of the causes of
unrest? Should we be willing to align ourselves with
extremists of left or right if that suits our
interests? Should we place our other interests at a
lower priority than the protection of human rights
throughout the world?

These are questions we must answer. It will not
be easy or quick. But we can simplify the discussion
if we answer the first question first: do any of our
international objectives warrant using the threat of
starting a nuclear war? If we can through discussion
reach a consensus on that question, we may find it
easier to agree on the subsequent questions, which can
be consolidated into a single question: What are we

prepared to give up, what price are we willing to pay, in order to defend our interests without having to launch a nuclear war?

Dealing with the Soviets

Both the preceding categories--nuclear weapons (particularly arms control negotiations) and international policies--involve dealing with the Soviets to reduce or eliminate the proximate causes of war, meaning those differences which could directly bring about U.S.-Soviet confrontation and war or speed up escalation to all-out war.

But there is another level, also important, at which U.S.-Soviet interaction must be given careful attention: the overall message that each receives from the other about long-range intentions. Each side, consciously or not, continually processes messages consisting of the other side's words and actions, and forms an overall impression of what the relationship is about. The American public's perceptions change from time to time, and are sometimes contradictory, but some attitudes seem firmly fixed at a consensus level: the Soviets will take advantage of us if we are weak, and you cannot trust the Russians. If an American is asked why he feels that way, he might be able to give specific reasons, but in fact the judgment is based on instinct growing out of accumulated "messages."

There is a similar judgment by Russians about Americans. We wonder how that could be, since our hearts are pure, but the fact that they are getting an unintended message illustrates how difficult it will be to change mutual perceptions of hostility. Aside from the difficulty of overcoming the natural inclination of national leaders to pursue immediate and marginal advantages at the expense of long-term objectives, it would require tolerance almost on a biblical scale to ask a nation to be conciliatory and sensitive to the sensibilities of another nation, if there seems to be no reciprocity.

In another era, proud and secure Americans could take the position that we need not go out of our way to worry about the sensibilities of others if they don't seem to worry about ours. But we, as well as the Soviets, have to take another look at the problem in light of the danger of nuclear oblivion that hangs over us.

The basic choice is between a "live-and-let-live" approach and an approach that says "eventually one or the other must give in, therefore we have to make sure it's they who change and not we." This is not an easy choice for Americans. We are predisposed to live and let live; we tolerate great diversity within our own society, and for the most part take pride in it. Yet we do not want to be taken for patsies. If pushed, we push back. We dislike despotism, and have no tolerance for bullies or those who try to use force to dominate others. On occasion we have shed our own blood precisely on that account.

The advent of large-scale nuclear arsenals forces us to reexamine the choices, however. If we truly believe it's either "us or them," that means we have to accept a significant risk that someday it will come to a nuclear showdown. The policy that flows from that judgment is self-evident. The "either us or them" approach is congruent with putting highest priority on "defending our interests" rather than on "avoiding nuclear war." But for some Americans it goes beyond the concept of risking nuclear war to defend against aggression; they define the continued existence of the Soviet Union in its present form as, in itself, a threat to our freedom.

The "live-and-let-live" approach, on the other hand, is roughly congruent with putting highest priority on avoiding nuclear war. It implies greater tolerance for accepting the continued existence of the Soviet Union in its present form, or in any other form it may evolve to, so long as it does not present a clear and imminent danger to us and our values. But even if the Soviet Union violates the "live-and-let-live" injunction, those who put highest priority on avoiding nuclear war would prescribe responding to Soviet provocations without using, or threatening to use, nuclear weapons, except in retaliation for Soviet use of them.

In any case, the problem is more complex than either of these two approaches suggests. Even apart from the nuclear issue, there are serious security concerns on both sides. We have military allies on their borders--Norway and Turkey--and have begun developing military ties with a country they regard as a true security threat in the long run, China. If they had their preferences, the Soviets would like a change in the status quo which moved some of what they perceive to be direct threats to their security farther from their borders, while retaining their alliance with Cuba, just off our shore, and their security position in Eastern Europe. Yet we and our friends and allies with justification regard Soviet rollback efforts as a threat to our security.

In these circumstances, a "live-and-let-live" attitude on our part will not be sufficient to move things in a safer direction if we define it as meaning that the Soviet Union must forever accept that its security in its own neighborhood cannot be improved. And a "live-and-let-live" attitude on their part will not help if they define it as meaning that we must accept changes in the security arrangements of the Soviet Union which put at risk our friends and allies.

These conflicting interests cannot be easily resolved, but it appears that they could more easily and safely be dealt with over time if each side were to act as if its highest priority were to avoid nuclear war, and recognized that an important path to that end is to develop confidence by each side that its vital interests are secure.

CONCLUSION

There is evidence that Americans are moving toward placing highest priority on avoiding nuclear war, but there is some question whether we are ready to begin dealing with the consequences of that choice: to take the tough decisions necessary to find other ways to protect our security and our interests around the world. If we take seriously the assumption behind President Reagan's Strategic Defense Initiative (SDI)--that we can effectively pursue our interests in a world where nuclear weapons have been abolished or rendered impotent--that would mean undertaking the research that will determine whether we can protect ourselves from nuclear weapons, but accepting constraints to assure that it does not take us down a dangerous path of no return. Meanwhile, we and our allies would make the necessary sacrifices to build up our non-nuclear defenses in order to reduce our reliance on nuclear weapons for defending ourselves against non-nuclear attack, with the goal of ending that reliance entirely as soon as possible. Our weapons and negotiating decisions would be made with that ultimate goal in mind. That long-term policy to end our reliance on nuclear weapons for anything but protecting against nuclear attack would force us to do hard thinking about our international policies--reexamining our interests and our goals, and taking a realistic view of what we must do to achieve them if we can no longer rely on nuclear threats.

Finally, we would begin the hard process of applying to relations with the Soviet Union our decision to put the highest priority on avoiding nuclear war. That would take time and patience, particularly in view of Soviet attitudes which will likely change only slowly, if at all. Although willingness to put one's self in the other fellow's shoes can help, we must not delude ourselves that this is merely a matter of getting to know each other better. There are vital interests at stake on either side, and the conflicts cannot be wished away. We can only resolve to deal with them calmly, and with a common recognition that we and the Soviets have one supreme, overriding common interest: the avoidance of nuclear war.

REFERENCES

Reagan interview with the <u>New York Times</u>, February 12, 1985.

Voter Options on Nuclear Arms Policy, The Public
    Agenda Foundation, New York, 1984, pp. 50-69.

Reagan Speech, March 23, 1983; Interview with the New
    York Times, February 12, 1985; "The Strategic
    Defense Initiative," Special Report No. 129, June
    1985, Department of State.

10

Managing Nuclear Proliferation: A Nonnuclear Response

Dagobert L. Brito and Michael D. Intriligator

There is an old story that many years ago, Khrushchev was reviewing the Soviet Armed Forces on May Day. It was a very impressive turnout. The Army marched by goosestepping in their polished jack boots, motorized infantry units drove by, the soldiers sitting at attention in their armored personnel carriers, the tank battalions rumbled past and the Strategic Rocket Forces displayed the latest missiles. After this impressive display of Soviet might came a few hundred middle-aged men. They were a scruffy-looking lot, their shoes weren't polished, some were overweight and balding, their suits looked as if they had been slept in, and there were soup stains on some of their ties. Shocked, Khrushchev turned to Brezhnev and asked, "Who are these people and what are they doing in our parade?" "Comrade," Brezhnev replied, "these are our economists. Never underestimate the damage they can do."

Having warned you, we would like to explain why economists and economics have anything to say about the subject of nuclear proliferation. Economists are trained to make reasonable assumptions about the objectives of economic agents and about the technology and resources at the disposal of these agents and then to work out the logical implications of these assumptions in order to analyze the workings of an economic system. Let us illustrate by example. Economics is known as the "dismal science," thanks to the work of the Reverend Thomas Robert Malthus. In 1798, he wrote an essay in which he predicted that the population would outstrip the supply of food. Malthus made two basic assumptions based on his observations of the world and then made a prediction. He assumed that the human population, if unchecked, would continue growing at a geometric rate so as to double every 25

This paper was written in 1985 and revised to reflect events that occurred in the spring of 1986. Our research on the arms race and the outbreak of war was supported by the National Science Foundation.

years. A geometric rate of growth leads to a sequence
like 2, 4, 8, 16, 32, 64, 128. He further assumed the
world's food production would continue growing, but
only at an arithmetic rate. An arithmetic rate of
growth leads to a sequence like 10, 11, 12, 13, 14, 15,
16. He predicted that at some point the two lines
would cross and mankind would face starvation. Malthus
was perhaps the first person to predict that two such
lines would cross in the future; as Dave Stockman would
no doubt agree, Malthus was not the last person to be
incorrect after making such a prediction.

But was Malthus wrong, and if so, why? Could he
have been expected to predict the tremendous advances
in American agriculture and in the technology that
first opened the prairie to cultivation and later gave
us new breeds of livestock and new varieties of crops,
technology that enabled us to increase food production
in order to keep up with population growth? Could he
have been expected to predict the dramatic improvements
in transportation technology which made it possible to
ship food economically from the new agricultural
regions to the rest of the world? We have only to
remember the vivid pictures of starving people in
Africa to realize that in those parts of the world
where Malthus' assumptions appear to be valid his
predictions appear, in fact, to be correct.

Our point in this brief excursion into economic
theory and history is to illustrate the role of the
economist in policy. The economist should not say:
"This will occur." Rather the economist should say:
"If this, then that."

ASSUMPTIONS

We will now make a few reasonable assumptions
about both the international environment and about the
agents who populate this environment; attempt to defend
these assumptions on theoretical and historical
grounds; derive the logical implications of these
assumptions; and then use these implications to make
some predictions concerning the proliferation of
nuclear weapons. We will not attempt to predict what
will happen in the next ten or fifteen years, but, like
Malthus, we will be presumptuous enough to deal in
decades.

Proposition 1: Wars Result From Rational Behavior

The first and most fundamental proposition is that
wars are usually the results of rational behavior on
the part of the agents involved.[1] This is not as strong
a proposition as it sounds. By "rational" we do not
mean that agents are wise or omniscient but simply that
when faced with a choice, they will take the option
they prefer. Further, rationality requires that their

choices be internally consistent, that is, that if an agent prefers option A to option B and option B to option C, he will not prefer option C to option A.

The second proposition is that in any society of individuals or nations there exists a stable relationship between the distribution of power and the distribution of wealth. If, for some reason, the distribution of power or of wealth is changed, conflict will occur until a new equilibrium is achieved. Theoretically, we can justify this proposition as the logical consequence of the first.

In game theory, there is a famous problem known as the "Nash Bargaining Problem." In it, two individuals meet and attempt to divide a good between them. Each has a threat in that he can unilaterally impose an allocation that can be dominated by an agreement. For example, there is a pie which the two individuals can divide between them if they can agree on its division; however, if they cannot agree, then each receives only a quarter piece of the pie. The one-quarter, one-quarter allocation is the "threat point."

In 1956, John Nash gave an axiomatic solution to this problem (Nash, 1956). He assumed a set of axioms which it was reasonable to impose on the solution, including such properties as rationality, feasibility, and symmetry. Nash showed that with these axioms the problem has a unique solution. In 1977, together with Buoncristiani, we worked out the logical implications of relaxing the symmetry axiom in the Nash Bargaining Problem (Brito, Buoncristiani, and Intriligator, 1977). We asked what would happen if the status quo was one of the determinants of a bargaining game with threats. In the pie example this means determining what would happen if before the bargaining started one person owned two-thirds of the pie and the other owned one-third. Could one party then use the threat of forcing both parties to consume only one-quarter of the pie by not agreeing to a distribution to force the other party to give him a bigger share? Would the status quo have any effect on the final distribution? We were able to show that it was possible to characterize the properties of the solution with a new set of axioms. We found that there were some distributions of power and wealth for which the status quo is the outcome of bargaining with threats but some other distributions of power and wealth for which bargaining with threats would result in a change of the distribution of wealth. Thus, there are some distributions of power and wealth which are stable and some which are not.

Axiomatic bargaining models are bloodless creatures; assumptions are made about the nature of the solution rather than about the behavior of the agents involved. They also do not allow you to study the cases in which an agreement may not be reached, since the results are based on axioms about the properties of the solution. To develop a deeper insight into the

role of threats in bargaining, we developed a formal
model of countries acting as rational agents in which
conflict, war, and redistribution may all occur (Brito,
and Intriligator, 1985). The countries are concerned
with economic rights to consumption in a two-period
model in which force can be used to redistribute these
rights. The first period of the model represents a
potential arms race in which countries choose between
consumption and investment in arms. The second period
of the model represents a period of potential crisis as
countries bargain and may use force or the threat of
force to attempt to reallocate resources. Again it was
possible to show that there are both distributions of
wealth and power which are stable and distributions of
wealth and power for which conflict and war may occur.

Proposition 2: The Relationship between Power and
Wealth Is Stable

If you accept our first fundamental proposition,
that wars are usually the results of rational behavior
on the part of the agents involved, then we would argue
that you should also accept our second proposition that
there is a stable relationship between power and the
distribution of wealth. Abstract theory, however, is a
nebulous creature, and it is difficult to expect
policy-makers to accept an argument--no matter how
sound--that depends on the continuity of a function in
an infinite-dimensional space.
     Let us attempt to make a historical argument for
the proposition that there is a stable relationship
between power and the distribution of wealth. An
important military innovation was the development of
disciplined heavy infantry by the Greek city-states.
This meant that battles were fought by military units
in which individuals supported each other rather than
acting as individual combatants. This required
training and discipline. The Greek city-states did not
have the economic base to maintain a large standing
army of professional soldiers so the army was manned by
citizens. Abroad, this innovation of disciplined heavy
infantry was translated into Greek military
predominance throughout the known world. At home, it
was consistent with the political rights of the
citizen-soldier. Although the causal flow is
uncertain, the distribution of power and the
distribution of rights within the city-state were in
equilibrium.
     The role of the citizen-soldier in the early Roman
Republic was similar to that in Greece. Infantry
tactics continued to evolve, and at Ausculum it was
demonstrated that legions were better that phalanxes.
The change came when the Romans were able to develop an
economic base sufficient to support professional
armies. Roman citizens soon lost certain political
rights as power shifted to the professional armies.

In the Middle Ages, the power of the medieval barons declined when the development of gunpowder and the expansion of the economic tax base enabled kings and burghers to demolish castles and field armies.

In relatively modern times Germany did not become a nation until 1870, after unification under Bismarck. The wealth and technology of the German empire made it the most powerful nation in Europe, yet by 1870, the pre-existing European powers had divided the colonial world among them, denying the Germans their "place in the sun." Power and the distribution of wealth were therefore no longer in equilibrium. The result: World Wars I and II.

These few examples do not "prove" that the proposition is correct; they do show that the proposition is plausible, especially since we have not been able to think of an example of a class or a country that was able to maintain its wealth and status despite the lack of political or military power.

Proposition 3:   Nuclear Technology Will Soon Be Widely Available

The final proposition we will make is about the evolution of technology. It is assumed that over the next 20 to 40 years the technology to build nuclear weapons will become available to most countries. Individuals who specialize in the economies and technologies of the countries involved believe that some 20 countries have the potential of acquiring nuclear weapons within the next decade. Their predictions are based on estimates of how long it would take these countries to acquire and to develop the ability to build nuclear weapons using existing technology.

Our ability to predict technological development 20 to 40 years in the future is probably no better than Malthus'. The number of people involved in research and development has grown faster than the population, which has itself grown geometrically. Twenty-five years ago no one would have predicted that the little computer we used to write this paper would be more powerful than virtually any computer that existed at the time. Thirty-five years ago no one would have predicted that the American automobile industry would be fighting competition from Japan and that American manufacturers would be importing radios from Singapore.

Ninety-five percent of the nations of the world in the year 1986 can probably duplicate the 1910 technological achievement of the United States. It is thus reasonable to assume that 95 percent of the nations of the world in the year 2020 will probably be able to duplicate the 1945 technological achievements of the United States. This proposition is reinforced by a recent Congressional Research Service report that "substantial numbers of (missiles) could be deployed in

most regions of the world in the not-too distant
future. The potential candidates for such deployment
include Israel, Syria, Egypt, Iraq, Libya, India,
Pakistan, Taiwan, South Korea, North Korea, Brazil and
Argentina." (emphasis added) (Houston Post, April 28,
1986).

Implications

If nations are rational agents, they will exploit
a situation if it is to their advantage. Nuclear
weapons are weapons of such power that they have not
been used since World War II; however, this does not
mean that they have not been useful. In an interview
on "Sixty Minutes" in January 1985, Arkady Shevchenko,
the highest ranking Soviet official to defect to the
US, stated that given its economic and technological
backwardness, the Soviet Union would be a second-rate
power without nuclear weapons. If he is correct, then
the acquisition of nuclear weapons by the Soviet Union
broke the link between the current determinants of its
wealth and its political power.

If nuclear weapons confer on their future
possessors a similar status to the one they have
conferred on the Soviet Union, then we face the
possibility that the relation between the distribution
of power and the present distribution of wealth would
no longer be stable. Policymakers in the year 2020 may
face an environment in which the implicit threat of the
use of nuclear weapons by Third World nations may
change the distribution of wealth by bargaining over
the terms of trade, patterns of aid, and other
determinants of the distribution of wealth.

We do not know what form this change would take:
whether the status quo powers would make political and
economic concessions to new nuclear powers to ensure
their political stability or whether the new nuclear
powers would feel able to engage in regional adventures
under the shield of their new nuclear umbrella. We can
only speculate, for example, whether Britain would have
risked a task force in the South Atlantic in the
Falklands War if Argentina had had the bomb or whether
the high probability that Israel is a nuclear power may
have influenced Egyptian President Anwar Sadat's peace
initiative (Schelling, 1983, and Brito and
Intriligator, 1983). Similarly, we can only speculate
whether a marginal Libyan nuclear force would have
deterred the United States from using force in April
1986. Libyan nuclear weapons would have increased
European pressure on the United States not to act. It
is possible that the United States would have had to
destroy the Libyan nuclear weapons; with the present
force structure, this would have been, at best, a risky
venture. We can only conclude that if nuclear weapons
can be translated into political power and if political
power is one of the determinants of the distribution of

wealth in the world, then nuclear proliferation will
change the distribution of wealth.

NUCLEAR NONPROLIFERATION

The above conclusion is of course based on a set
of assumptions; if any of these assumptions is not
valid, then the conclusion is not valid. A different
conclusion can be reached by making a different set of
assumptions. For example, assume that in the next
forty years (1) the nature of man will change and
nations will not use force when it is to their
advantage; (2) there is no relation between power and
the distribution of wealth; (3) the nuclear nations
will be able to keep the less-developed countries from
acquiring the necessary technology.
     Of the three contrapositive assumptions, we find
only the third remotely plausible, and in fact, it is
one of the assumptions on which current U.S. policy is
based. The difficulty we see with this is that many of
the technical innovations that will probably make it
feasible for the less-developed nations to build
nuclear weapons also have legitimate peaceful
applications. For example, a major obstacle in the
building of a nuclear bomb is the difficulty (because
of its extreme toxicity) in machining plutonium, but
this difficulty can be overcome via computer controlled
machine tools that do not require human operators.
These tools can be acquired by a potential nuclear
power for perfectly legitimate reasons.
     This analysis suggests that perhaps one of the
most promising ways to avoid a world with a multitude
of nuclear powers is to break the link between nuclear
weapons and national power. This can be accomplished
by the carrot and the stick, via incentives provided
and costs imposed by the nuclear powers. Incentives
could, for example, be based on international aid to
the less-developed nations that refrain from nuclear
weapons development.
     An alternative way of managing nuclear
proliferation is to reduce the importance of nuclear
weapons. Nuclear weapons are a strategic anomaly.
Liddell-Hart, in his history of World War II, argued
that the doctrine of strategic bombing evolved simply
to justify the existence of an independent Royal Air
Force (Liddell-Hart, 1970: 589-612). General Hugh
Trenchard was a leading advocate of the theory that
airpower could be used "as a means of direct attack on
the enemy state with the object of depriving it of the
means or will to continue the war." In the United
States, General William Mitchell was the leading
advocate of this theory. They felt that airpower could
be used to destroy the enemy's capacity to wage war.
Unfortunately, they were ahead of their time.
     Attempts to use aircraft as strategic weapons in
World War II were expensive and not very effective. In

April 1941 the theoretical error of drop was assumed to
be 1,000 yards, but the Butt report in 1941 stated
that during raids on the Ruhr only one-tenth of the
bombs fell within five miles of their targets. In May
1942, 1,046 bombers were used to destroy 600 acres of
the city of Cologne, but at the cost of forty bombers.
In June 1942 Bremen was attacked by 904 bombers which
inflicted little damage and lost 5 percent of the
bomber force. With loss rates like this, a bomber crew
had one chance in eight of surviving forty missions.
Despite the fact that 200,000 tons of bombs were
dropped on Germany in 1943, production rose by 50
percent.

It is not surprising, therefore, that in the
context of the times the goal of bombing changed from
destroying the enemy's ability to fight to destroying
the enemy's morale. The result was the attacks on the
populations of Hamburg, Dresden, and Tokyo. The
decision to use the atomic bomb is still a subject of
some controversy; however, it was in many ways a
logical extension of existing practices (Giovannitti
and Freed, 1965: 38). The atomic bomb was an
economical and efficient means of destroying cities,
industries, and the enemy's will to fight. It did not
do anything that was not already being done by both
sides in the war.

There were two developments at that time, however,
which have been largely overlooked in the postwar
development of strategic doctrine. The first was the
effectiveness of the raids in 1944 against German oil
production. By September 1944, German fuel production
was reduced to 10,000 tons a month, while the Luftwaffe
needed 160,000 tons a month to operate. Albert Speer,
Hitler's minister of armaments, was able to build
fighter planes, but the Germans did not have the fuel
to fly them or to train pilots (Speer, 1970: 346-61).
Modern economies are vulnerable to disruptions in fuel,
transportation, and communications. Developing
economies, inasmuch as they tend to be more
centralized, are even more so. A tragic example was
the near paralysis of communications in central Mexico
after the 1985 earthquake destroyed the telephone
exchange in Mexico City.

The second development was the effectiveness of
the V-2 against British morale. Although the German
rocket attacks on England did not cause as much actual
damage as the Blitz, the blow to British morale was
devastating. Being attacked and being able to fight
may actually unite a people against an attacker; being
attacked without being able to respond may be
psychologically cataclysmic.

Recent technological developments now make it
possible to use conventional warheads "as a means of
direct attack on the enemy state with the object of
depriving it of the means or will to continue the war."
In 1945 and in 1965 the United States did not have the
ability to cripple a country by precise non-nuclear

bombing. In 1985 it has a technology which can deliver
warheads to within a few hundred feet. It should be
possible for the United States to develop by 1995 the
capability of attacking and destroying with
conventional explosives and without endangering
aircrews such critical targets as oil refineries,
airports, waterworks, electrical generation plants,
military bases, and nuclear reactors.

Possibly the most efficient ways to accomplish
this task are the cruise missile and the ballistic
missile. Cruise missile technology is still under
development, so it is difficult to speculate on how it
would evolve if attempts were made to develop a
conventional strategic weapon based on this technology.
Ballistic missile technology, however, has reached the
point where it is possible to speculate on the
characteristics of such a weapon using published
parameters.

A conventionally armed ballistic missile (CABM)
that weighs 80,000 pounds and can carry a payload in
the neighborhood of 12,000 to 18,000 pounds with a
range of 1,000 miles is probably feasible. A CABM this
size could be based on submarines. For example, the
Trident I C-4, weighs 70,000 pounds and the Trident II
D-5 weighs 126,000 pounds. If such a CABM were to be
as accurate as the proposed Midgetman, it would have a
CEP (Circular Error Probable) of .05 miles. The
warhead can be designed as appropriate for the target.
Cluster bombs could be used against soft targets such
as airfields; heavier, armor-piercing warheads can be
used against reinforced structures such as nuclear
reactors. A warhead that carried 16,000 pounds of
explosives would be equivalent to more than eight
16-inch shells or almost 17 salvos from a 155 mm
battery. Against soft targets, this would be enough to
destroy almost four square kilometers. Six to eight
CABMS would have been sufficient to accomplish the
mission of the April 1986 attack on Libya (Aviation
Week, April 21, 1986).

The CABM carrier could be a conventionally powered
submersible. To satisfy arms control considerations,
it would be desirable that the Soviets be able to
verify that the CABM does not have a nuclear warhead.
If the CABM carrier were conventionally powered, the
Soviets could verify by airborne detectors that there
were not any nuclear weapons on board when the vessel
was on the surface. The British experience in the
Falklands War suggests that it would be useful to be
able to defend the CABM carrier from air-launched
missile attacks by secondary naval powers. If it were
a submersible, it could dive if attacked by air.

The existence of such a weapon would reduce the
temptation of non-nuclear nations to acquire nuclear
weapons. Threats to use it would be credible and would
not be conditional on the consent of third parties.
The nuclear weapons program of a country tempted to
make political use of its nuclear weapons would always

be at risk of a non-nuclear first strike.   It would be necessary for that country to harden its nuclear weapons before they would be useful; not acquiring them could well be a more attractive and less expensive alternative.

CONCLUSION

In this essay we have attempted to use economic reasoning to address the problem of nuclear proliferation.   Three propositions were posed: (1) nations will use force when it is to their advantage; (2) there is a relation between power and the distribution of wealth; (3) in the next 40 years the nuclear nations will not be able to keep the less-developed countries from acquiring the necessary technology.   These propositions were used to argue that nuclear proliferation could lead to a fundamental change in the distribution of wealth in the world. Indeed, it could be argued that the existence of nuclear weapons has already created an arena in which the minor powers have been able to exploit the superpower rivalry to obtain economic and political concessions.   An obvious example is Cuba.   A possible means of addressing this problem is for the United States to deploy a force of conventionally armed cruise or ballistic missiles which would serve to deter proliferation and to act as a counter to the political use of nuclear weapons by the nations that do acquire them.
This is not to suggest that the developed nations do not have some responsibility toward the rest of the world.   Aid to the less-developed nations for economic development could be part of a program to manage nuclear proliferation by reducing the need for such weapons.   However, economic redistribution under explicit nuclear duress is not likely to lead to a more "just" global distribution of wealth and has the potential of being a catalyst for superpower conflict.

NOTES

1.   See Bueno de Mesquita (1981) for a discussion and defense of this assumption.   He also uses this assumption to analyze past wars.   The details of his study are controversial, but he is persuasive in arguing that wars are consistent with rational decision making.   Of the 58 major wars fought since the Congress of Vienna, the initiator won 42 of them.   Bueno de Mesquita argues that if wars were nonrational events, then there would be no systematic relationship between the initiator of a war and the victor.   Using the historical record, he computed that such an event could have occured at random only 1 in 2,500 times.   He also computed benefit/cost ratios and found that when wars

have occurred, it was usually in the interest of one
party.

2.   Missile parameters were published in Jane's
Fighting Ships 1984-85, Collins (1985), and the New
York Times, April 26, 1986. The Minute Man III weighs
78,000 pounds and has a throw-weight of 2,400 pounds
and a range of 8000 miles. There are not enough
published parameters available to provide sufficient
boundary conditions to solve the orbital equations, so
range/payload approximations were computed by
assuming conservation of energy of the payload outside
the atmosphere. A rough assumption is that the product
of the throw-weight and range are constant. This
assumption implies, for a missile similar to the
Minuteman III, a throw-weight of 4,800 pounds at a
range of 4,000 miles, a throw-weight of 9,600 pounds at
a range of 2,000 miles, and a throw-weight of 19,200
pounds at a range of 1,000 miles.

REFERENCES

Aviation Week and Space Technology, April 21, 1986.

Brito, D. L., A. M. Buoncristiani and M. D.
    Intriligator (1977), "A New Approach to the Nash
    Bargaining Problem," Econometrica 45: 1163-72.

Brito, D. L., and M. D. Intriligator (1985), "Conflict,
    War and Redistribution," American Political
    Science Review 79: 943-57.

Brito, D. L., and M. D. Intriligator (1983),
    "Proliferation and the Probability of War: Global
    and Regional Issues," in D. L. Brito, M. D.
    Intriligator, and A. E. Wick, eds., Strategies for
    Managing Nuclear Proliferation--Economic and
    Political Issues, 135-43, Lexington: Lexington
    Books.

Bueno de Mesquita, B. (1971), The War Trap, New
    Haven: Yale University Press.

Collins, J. M.   (1985), U.S.-Soviet Military Balance,
    1980- 1985, New York: Pergamon-Brassey's.

Gabriel, R. A. (1985), Military Incompetence, New
    York: Hill & Wang.

Giovannitti, L., and F. Freed (1965), The Decision to
    Drop the Bomb, New York: Coward-McCann, Inc.

Houston Post, April 28, 1986.

Jane's Fighting Ships 1984-85, London: Jane's
    Publishing Company, Limited.

Liddell-Hart, B. H. (1970), History of the Second
    World War, New York: G. P. Putnam's Sons.

Nash, J. F. (1956), "The Bargaining Problem,
    Econometrica 18: 155-62

New York Times, April 26, 1986.

Schelling, T. C. (1983), "Comments," in D. L. Brito,
    M. D. Intriligator and A. E. Wick, eds.,
    Strategies for Managing Nuclear Proliferation--
    Economic and Political Issues, 156-58, Lexington:
    Lexington Books.

Speer, A. (1970), Inside the Third Reich, New York:
    Macmillan Publishing Co., Inc.

11

SDI and Nuclear Weapons: The Need for a Nuclear Freeze

Stephen Hoffius

For several decades, the main change in Soviet and American nuclear weapons policy has been to build more and to build better. Each country's new technological developments have been quickly copied by the other. Instead of becoming more secure, our countries--in fact, all countries--have become more uncertain of our security, more threatened. We are threatened both by the numbers of weapons we have developed and by their design.

MORE AND BETTER WEAPONS

The United States now possesses approximately 25,000 nuclear warheads. (Almost 2,000 warheads are stored right here in South Carolina, more than in any other state.) The Soviet Union has between 23,000 and 33,000. Britain, France, and China have each produced hundreds. Other countries, including Israel, probably control nuclear weapons. And many more--South Africa, Libya, Pakistan, and India, among others--have shown great interest in acquiring nuclear stockpiles.

There are more than 50,000 nuclear warheads in the world today. According to Nuclear Battlefields, published by the Institute for Policy Studies, these warheads,

> most smaller than suitcases, can each obliterate cities. Just a few can kill millions of people and destroy the environment for decades hence. The smallest smallest nuclear warheads are ten times more powerful than the largest conventional weapons. The largest have the power of forty billion pounds of conventional explosives. (p. 37)

The Congressional Quarterly book U.S. Foreign Policy: The Reagan Imprint describes our most recently developed weapons as "more compact, easily concealed,

accurate and effective than those of the past." (p. 35)
The Pershing IIs, which the United States deployed in
Europe in late 1983, are able to reach targets in the
western part of the Soviet Union in just 10 to 12
minutes. Imagine the response of United States
officials if we learned that the Soviet Union could
destroy American cities and defense facilities with
such little notice. Imagine weapons of this accuracy
and speed in, for instance, Cuba or Nicaragua.
American citizens would be frightened and furious and
would demand that this initiative be countered at once.
We must assume that the Soviet Union is doing the same.

THE PRESIDENT'S RESPONSE

Every American President has had to face the
threat that nuclear weapons pose to the world. Though
all since Truman have succeeded in avoiding their use,
none has been able to eliminate their threat. Each
President has set limits that have allowed for
continual arsenal growth and development, making a
dangerous situation even worse.
President Reagan's approach to this threat has
been unique. He has dismissed major Soviet arms
reduction proposals almost as soon as they have been
made. He did not meet with his Soviet counterparts
throughout his entire first term of office. And rather
than face the issue of nuclear weapons today, he has
said instead that we will develop the Strategic Defense
Initiative (SDI), which he claims could lead to their
elimination in the next century. His administration
has told us, essentially, not to worry about the 50,000
nuclear warheads in our midst. Let your children and
grandchildren worry about them. As Ambassador Kenneth
Adelman has made clear, the development of SDI is the
cornerstone of the President's efforts towards arms
control and disarmament. President Reagan has even
refused to consider limiting his "Star Wars" plans for
the future in exchange for major cuts in nuclear
weapons today.
For the next few decades, SDI will consist mostly
of laboratory work and computer modeling. It cannot
possibly lead to arms reductions. Instead, it will
trigger two new arms races. The Soviet Union has
accurately described SDI as having first strike
potential. If the United States continues with its
plans, the Soviet Union will inevitably attempt to
produce a nominally defensive program of its own. In
addition, the Soviet Union will attempt to develop
offensive weapons which cannot be detected by a
space-based defense. And, of course, the United States
will do the same.
Scientists and engineers, at least, should be
ecstatic. Star Wars research could provide them with
even more funding than did the Manhattan Project during
World War II or the original NASA push of the early

1960s. The preliminary SDI research alone will cost at
least 26 billion dollars over five years. Some
observers estimate that its price will eventually rise
to a trillion dollars. The Pentagon is hardly noted
for its frugality. In the meantime, because of our
national deficit, Congress and President Reagan have
demanded cutbacks in those government programs which
provide people with their basic necessities: food,
health care, housing, education, and job training. But
Star Wars, we are told, is too important to cut from
the budget.

THE STRATEGIC DEFENSE INITIATIVE AND NUCLEAR WEAPONS

Thousands of American scientists doubt that SDI
could ever work, certainly not to the level of
perfection necessary for true security. Edward Teller,
who, according to news reports, first suggested "Star
Wars" to President Reagan, has admitted that "a great
number of American scientists, perhaps the majority,"
oppose SDI. And no wonder. No other scientific or
engineering system--no computer or power station, no
missile or space shuttle--has ever worked as well and
as quickly as this system will have to work. Never
before have we placed such trust in a scientific
system. And yet, despite its importance, the Strategic
Defense Initiative, by its very nature, can never be
fully tested. Politicians are making the American
people suffer needlessly for a weapons system that may
never work.

It is a mistake, I think, if we let President
Reagan turn our attention entirely from nuclear weapons
to SDI. The Strategic Defense Initiative is rooted in
the Reagan Administration's ability to deal effectively
with the threat of nuclear weapons. The President
expects the Soviet Union to cut its offensive weapons,
while we, in exchange, will cut nothing. Instead, we
will develop a defensive system with the potential for
offensive uses. He still does not recognize that the
problem is not simply their bombs, nor our bombs, but
all nuclear weapons.

While scientists theorize and debate, 50,000
nuclear weapons remain deployed around the world.
Though just 10 or 12 minutes separate us from
annihilation, President Reagan hopes his SDI system
could be in place in just a few decades. Then--and
only then--will we be allowed to think of the
elimination of nuclear weapons. We don't have the time
to wait.

For though Kenneth Adelman boasts that we have
enjoyed 39 years without a major war, those years have
hardly been peaceful. In the Korean War, more than
100,000 soldiers of South Korea, the United States and
other United Nations forces were killed, in addition to
a million and a half people from China and North Korea.
In the war in Vietnam, a million South Vietnamese were

killed, and perhaps the same number of North
Vietnamese. Almost 60,000 Americans never came home.
And there have been scores of other wars and
revolutions in Asia, Africa, Latin America, South
America, and the Middle East.

If Adelman thinks a war with two million deaths is
not "major," it is only because those 50,000 warheads
have changed our definition of the term. For some
time, we have known that all life on this planet could
be destroyed by the radiation resulting from a massive
exchange of nuclear weapons. Now scientists studying
the possibility of "nuclear winter" have demonstrated
that even what we once called a "limited" nuclear war
would trigger climatic changes that could leave the
earth as barren as the moon. It is something many
people expect. And when it doesn't happen, we rejoice.
We have to. Because the next major war, which could
take place while work on the Strategic Defense
Initiative (SDI) continues, will make all previous wars
appear minor. There will be far more victims. And we
will all be among them.

12

SDI: Renewing an American Tradition

Jamie W. Moore

President Ronald Reagan's program for a Strategic
Defense Initiative (SDI) has its origins in the
continuing effort of intellectuals in the defense
community to break free from the paradoxes resulting
from the search for security through the acquisition of
nuclear arms. Upon coming to office in 1981, the
Reagan Administration found itself looking at two broad
national security policies. One began with the
consideration of military systems and incorporated
diplomacy, the other started with diplomatic goals and
incorporated military systems to attain them. Both had
origins in events immediately following World War II.

EVOLUTION OF NUCLEAR DETERRENCE

   Nuclear weapons changed the nature of war in 1945.
By the early 1950s, the acquisition of small nuclear
arsenals gave both America and Russia the ability to
deliver a near-instantaneous attack which threatened to
incapacitate the opponent. The only rational military
policy was one which called for the possession but not
the use of nuclear weapons--Deterrence. Deterrence
required the United States to be able to restrain
Russian leaders from aggression, permanently, by
maintaining a capacity to destroy the Soviet Union no
matter what else occurred. In concrete terms, this
meant preparing to attack Russian cities. The first
element in creating the deterrence system was to
acquire the large numbers of weapons, delivery
vehicles, and command and control systems to be able to
execute the strike. The second was to devise ways to
protect the U.S. system so that enough of it could
survive a Soviet attack to devastate Russia.
Preserving the capability to deter became the primary
objective in American national security thought.
Because the United States Air Force provided the
principal deterrence system, protecting it from the
growing stockpile of Soviet nuclear bombs and delivery
systems assumed overriding importance.

In the 1950s, perceptions of a rapidly increasing Russian capacity to destroy the Strategic Air Command in a preemptive strike, spurred on by intelligence efforts that overestimated Soviet capabilities, led the United States to acquire weapons and delivery systems faster. This activity spewed out a profusion of plans about their use in wartime. To confer rationality upon the multiple targeting which had occurred in the various armed service programs, a Strategic Integrated Operating Plan (SIOP-62, 1960) was adopted. But it had a major drawback in that the imprecision in employing a nuclear weapons meant that in the circumstances of an actual or impending Soviet attack against Western Europe, the United States planned to unload the entire strategic alert force of 1,459 nuclear bombs against 654 targets in Russia, China, and Eastern Europe, whether the latter were involved in the crisis or not (Kaplan, Wizzards of Armageddon). What was needed was a new strategic concept, one which offered American leaders other options in the use of nuclear weapons.

COUNTER FORCE STRATEGY

A doctrinal variation on Deterrence was developed. Called Counterforce, it was founded on a proposition that the United States could employ nuclear weapons in limited ways and at lower levels and thereby avoid a situation where in a crisis a President would have to choose between a nuclear holocaust and doing nothing. In concrete terms, Counterforce meant attacking Russian strategic systems instead of cities. The problem with Counterforce was that it called for conducting wars with a calculation and precision heretofore absent from conflicts between great powers, and no one was certain nuclear weapons could be employed in such a sophisticated fashion (National Security Defense Memorandum-242, 1973; Presidential Directive-59, 1980).

Meanwhile, the rush to acquire weapons and systems for strategic defense had spawned an arms race which, proceeding upward through a number of levels, left the superpowers less secure than ever. An important question now was whether the Soviet Union or the nuclear arms race was the greater menace to American security.

CONTROLLING THE ARMS RACE

Controlling the arms race involved two kinds of diplomatic initiatives. One was to negotiate with the Soviet Union to slow the race to acquire new weapons and delivery systems. This involved the difficult business of identifying parity between the two superpowers and accepting it in a written treaty (SALT I, 1972; SALT II, 1980). The second (Detente) posited that maintaining close connections with the Soviet

Union at as many levels as possible would lead both
superpowers to work together in a common interest to
see that small crises did not escalate into
life-threatening confrontations.

Neither diplomatic alternative had broad
philosophical or political appeal because both
explicitly stated that the tension between the United
States and the Soviet Union was a permanent fact of
international life, at least as far as one could
foresee. They required the United States to recognize
officially that it could only employ its military
arsenal defensively, as opposed to forcing changes in
Russian policy. Agreements reached had to accept the
status quo of a continued Soviet threat. For many
people they were, at best, a less bad choice than an
accelerating arms race.

DEFENSIVE STRATEGIES

What the Reagan Administration and a significant
number of the American people wanted was a defense
system which protected the United States and freed it
to conduct foreign and military policies which would
negate the Russian threat. The Strategic Defense
Initiative (SDI) was the administration's answer. This
was an astute choice. Large numbers of scientists and
defense experts could question the efficacy of SDI on a
broad range of grounds, beginning with whether it could
be made to work at all, but this would not matter much.
For reasons to be noted later, SDI tapped deep roots in
American society. The administration could be assured
it would gain broad public support.

Early American history is a record of strategic
vulnerability. The Anglo-American colonists relied
upon a militia to deal with Indians and threats from
neighboring colonial settlements. For defense against
major Dutch, French, or Spanish assaults, they depended
upon England's navy. The War for Independence turned
that British fleet against them, and during the
American Revolution, with the exception of the Battle
of Yorktown, the Royal Navy commanded the seas,
transporting and supplying the armies which controlled
important reaches of the North American coast. An
inability to defend against an oceanborn attact was a
fact of American existence after independence was won.
When the French Revolution bequeathed a series of major
wars that buffeted the young Republic, Americans,
against the theme of their revolutionary
pronouncements, reestablished a standing army and navy
and adopted permanent military institutions and a
bureaucratic apparatus to support them. In the War of
1812, the British again projected large expeditionary
forces onto the American mainland, revealing the
inadequacy of America's defenses.

National Security Based on Fortifications

A "national security" policy followed quickly. It
originated in 1816 when Congress, at the specific
request of President James Madison, commissioned Simon
Bernard, Marshal of France and former Chief of
Artillery to Napoleon, a Brigadier General in the
United States Army and simultaneously established a
Board of Engineers for Fortifications for him to head.
The board was to design and oversee the construction of
a comprehensive system of coastal fortifications. In
addition to carrying out its assigned duty, during the
first decade of its existence the Fortifications Board
compiled a coherent body of thought which it then used
to justify its programs to Congress. There were two
basic propositions. The first combined the idea of
America's uniqueness with a distrust of foreigners.
Because the United States was an independent republic
and the leader in a democratic movement which was
transforming the world, European monarchies could not
and would not tolerate the continued existence of the
United States. They awaited only the right moment to
strike. Their attack would come suddenly and without
warning. The second proposition doubted both the
commitment of Americans to their society and the
ability of republicans to sustain themselves in a long
struggle. If the people faced a harsh crisis or had to
suffer through a prolonged war without the protection
of emplaced defenses, it held, they would capitulate to
an enemy rather than continue. Both axioms led to the
conclusion that American defenses had to be in place
before war came. Congress funded construction of the
fortifications system, thereby accepting the defense
concepts, but insisted on oversight authority and was
not generous with funding.

In the period between the War of 1812 and the
outbreak of the Civil War, military men sought to
establish themselves as members of a unique profession
which carried with it the authority to define their
appropriate areas of activity. They contended that
civilians should make the political decisions, that
military men should give military advice and not
address political questions (and, when asked, would
conduct military affairs), and that civilians and
military alike should respect each other's spheres. By
the 1850s, military men were speaking with more
authority on defense questions and their opinions were
being accepted more readily. Military strategists
expressed alarm at the impact on American security of
the swift pace of industrialization, with the constant
innovations in military technology, and the parallel
increase in the ability of foreign governments to
organize their peoples for wars. They warned that
America was in greater danger than before. To them,
the lesson of the Crimean War was that Great Britain
had the capacity to raise an army, land it on another
continent, and wage a successful campaign. They argued

that threats to the United States could no longer be
measured by the size of foreign armies and navies but
should be judged by the capacity of foreign governments
to expand their forces in wartime. Somewhat persuaded
that the United States had to prepare to defend against
armies and fleets an enemy might raise up, Congress now
spent more generously for a shield defense.
Approximately one-third of all funds expended for
coastal fortifications between the War of 1812 and the
Civil War were appropriated between 1850 and 1860.

The Civil War was not the crisis foreseen by the
defense strategists. The state-of-the-art casemated
fortifications, the major component of the defense
system, were battered down by rifled cannon. The Union
and the Confederacy raised up armies whose size and
striking power laid to rest any doubts about the
ability of the United States to repel a foreign
invasion. Americans in the North and the South
demonstrated a ferocious tenacity to their causes and a
determination to see the war to a victorious
conclusion.

All this notwithstanding, defense advocates
shortly were taking the pre-Civil War principles of
defense and fitting them into the modern industrial
world. By the latter decades of the nineteenth
century, certain that a number of technological
problems had been solved or soon would be, they began
pressing Congress to construct a new system of coastal
fortifications. The Endicott Fortifications Board and
phalanxes of civilian advocates worked to convince the
American people and Congress that the relative
inferiority of the United States to European powers in
the numbers of ships afloat, warship tonnage, guns at
sea, land fortifications, guns in place ashore, and men
under arms constituted a clear and present danger. A
threat could arise in the future quickly, they warned,
and the United States had to be ready when it did. The
favorite lessons of history employed in support of the
new defense program were the effective resistance of
Fort Sumter during the Civil War, the bombardment of
Alexandria by a British fleet in 1882, and the French
experience in the Franco-Prussian War (1870). Lumped
together, this trilogy proved that enemies could
prepare in secret and strike suddenly from the sea and
that nations which did not erect defenses in peacetime
would be overwhelmed by well-prepared aggressors before
they could react. The defense community identified the
British as the major threat to the United States,
predicted armed vessels steaming from Halifax and
arriving at major American cities within 36 hours, and
warned that a hostile fleet, by threatening great
damage--estimated as being equivalent to the Chicago
fire of 1871 which destroyed over $200 million in
property--could put an enemy in a position to humiliate
the United States. Between 1879 and 1914, the United
States constructed the requested fortifications system.

Military and naval officers also refined their concepts of professionalism. Army officers like Emory Upton argued militantly that the profession of arms required a lifetime of study and dedication, that the planning and conduct of war were activities too important to be left to civilian amateurs, and advised the rapid professionalization of the armed services and changes in the decision-making processes which would put military men nearer the center of national and foreign policy formulation.

The U.S. Navy as a Defensive Shield

The most widely read and quoted authority of the period, Alfred Thayer Mahan, gave similar advice, but in a setting more congenial to a less alarmed national audience. He offered a coherent, fully developed system of naval thought which married a strategy for defense with a formula for commercial development and prosperity. Mahan located in historical analogies the elements which governed the rise and fall of modern nations, the universal military principles that applied to the handling of troops or vessels in combat, and the relationships among industrial development, economic growth, and overseas trade and commerce. He concluded that war, especially for economic and commercial advantage, was an inescapable part of the human condition, and, on the basis of his evidence, advised that the United States needed a modern battleship fleet to protect the merchant marine, the overseas trade routes, and American vital interests. The navy Mahan recommended went under construction in the 1880s, could show the flag by 1895, fought a victorious war against Spain in 1898, and by 1905 had grown to become the world's third-largest fleet, with responsibilities to defend continental North America and possessions overseas.

The Endicott fortifications system was never called upon to defend America or deter aggressors. Examination of foreign archives reveals no serious plans in any capital to attack the United States. The outbreak of World War I and the circumstances of American entry into the conflict bore no resemblance to the dangers warned of by the turn of the century defense thinkers.

At the conclusion of the First World War, though not safe for democracy, the world was fairly safe for a United States which faced no formidable overseas enemies. The enlarged American navy was then the equal of any afloat. Naval strength, the absence of any readily discernible threat, and the security offered by two broad oceans contributed to a defense concept founded on continued expenditures for coastal fortifications and naval expansion, an updating of pre-World War I ideas.

Between the wars, strategists wrestled with three related and fundamental questions. The first, important between 1919 and 1935, was how to resolve the conflict inherent in the fact that the United States simultaneously was practicing economic internationalism and professing political isolation. The second, important from 1936 to 1939, had to do with the means--political, economic, military, moral--the United States could employ to influence overseas events. When World War II broke out in 1939, the question of defining the overseas frontier of American defense presented itself. The two-decade debate was conducted against the backdrop of a near-unanimous domestic consensus that the United States would be isolated from the conflict itself. People felt the nation had no business in any more European wars, their leaders were reassured by the fact the power balances in Europe and Asia favored American interests. Even in the later 1930s, France's army, the British fleet, and the broad Atlantic Ocean all stood between the United States and any Nazi menace. Japan, Russia, and China checked each other on the Asian mainland, while in the Pacific the United States, Great Britain, France, and the Netherlands possessed enough weight to counterbalance Japan.

The End of No Standing Alliances

The world became a far more dangerous place in 1940 with the fall of France. Great Britain, weakened and alone, faced Germany and Italy. Japan moved more boldly in Asia. Only a negligible few Americans now questioned the need to acquire stronger defenses. The issue was whether American security required aiding allies, at the risk of becoming involved in the war, or depended upon the construction in the Western Hemisphere of a Fortress America defended by much larger military, naval, and air forces. With military and naval leaders in agreement, and sometimes leading the way, the administration proceeded along the internationalist course, finding innovative ways to send rapidly increasing quantities of material overseas and expanding the 1930s policy of perimeter defense of the Western Hemisphere into a policy of all aid to potential allies short of war. Deterrence was practiced in the Pacific. Called "watchful waiting," the strategy meant that the United States so firmly opposed Japan's aims in China and Southeast Asia that it would station the American Pacific Fleet at Pearl Harbor, thereby forcing the Japanese to cease their aggression by confronting them with an impasse resolvable only when they changed their policies. America could wait until they did.

After the Japanese attack at Pearl Harbor, Americans turned their backs on the tradition of no entangling alliances, political non-intervention, and

dreams of an American destiny independent of other
nations and fought a global war as a leading member of
the Allied coalition. The experience of World War II
taught American defense planners three important
lessons. The first was that prior to the German attack
on the Soviet Union (June 1941), the balance of world
military power had passed into the hands of four
totalitarian states (Germany, Italy, Japan, and Russia)
who were bound together in a series of treaties and
agreements, and the Western democracies could not have
prevailed against this coalition. This condition was
too dangerous to be allowed to occur again. The second
lesson was that aggressor states could not be appeased.
One could not do business with a Hitler. The final
lesson was that the United States had to be
semi-mobilized. In the future, there would be no time
to create defenses out of a peacetime society after a
crisis occurred.

POST-WORLD WAR II SECURITY POLICY

The post-World War II national security policy
recommendations (NSC-68, 1950) were laid down after
events of the early Cold War years convinced American
leaders that the Soviet Union was aggressive and
powerful and a real threat to American ideals. The
outbreak of the Korean War (1950) became the vehicle to
implement them.

The development of basic national security
concepts and their evolution, described above,
followed. The results, as noted, were not all that
satisfactory. Rather than bringing security, adding
more nuclear weapons made the world a more dangerous
place in which to live. Diplomacy could not lead to
the clear-cut and favorable resolution of outstanding
problems.

These realities, of course, reflected the nature
of the world after 1945 and the limits of American
power within it. But this was a new world,
uncomfortable to Americans soaked in an ethos nurtured
during decades when there had been real security. By
recalling the elements of national security systems
before the Second World War, the Strategic Defense
Initiative held out the promise of regaining what had
been lost. America had contemplated powerful enemies
overseas before. In the past, rapidly advancing
technology had threatened a risky future. But previous
generations had found answers to these problems. It
would not matter that two prior national security
systems based on fortifications had proved irrelevant
to the challenges the United States would face and that
a third system employing the navy as a shield and a
deterrence threat had not worked. Supporting Star
Wars, modern Americans could find their way back to
normalcy.

13

Conclusion

W. Gary Nichols and Milton L. Boykin

When The Citadel Symposium on Arms Control and Nuclear
Weapons took place in February 1985, the nuclear
weapons race between the Soviet Union and the United
States seemed effectively out of control. In Geneva
and Vienna, talks aimed at resolving at least some of
the aspects of the competition had floundered and
prospects for positive achievements appeared bleak. A
subsequent summit meeting in Geneva failed to produce
any significant changes, and stepped-up efforts on both
sides to achieve technological advantages over the
other further diminished hopes for an agreement to
limit their ominous competition.

On the one hand, the essays in this volume clearly
reflect these unpromising conditions. On the other
hand, they propose general and more specific actions
which could end the nuclear arms race, prevent the
proliferation of these weapons, and reduce steadily the
enormous numbers of them on both sides. General George
Seignious believes that the asymmetrical nature of each
of the two powers' nuclear forces has made comparisons
of strength difficult. As a result, he says, each side
feels less secure and more eager to strenghten its
advantages vis-a-vis the other, thereby intensifying
the dangerous asymmetrical relationship between their
nuclear forces. Professor Larry Addington makes much
the same points, emphasizing, as does Seignious, the
contrasting need for symmetry and balance of forces
from which the two powers could begin reciprocal and
equitable reductions. A major figure in the SALT II
Accords, Seignious asserts that the great value of the
agreement lay not only in limiting the number of
weapons and warheads on each side, but also in
establishing this same equitable and symmetrical
balance between the nuclear force structures of both
sides. Most unfortunately, as he recounts, domestic
political issues wrecked ratification of the agreement
in the Senate and created at best a fractured framework
for future negotiations. Nevertheless, Seignious and
Addington clearly show that we must begin with a
symmetry and balance of nuclear forces, and remain

there, before we can end with their limitation and
elimination.

Certainly there are dangers and obstacles along
this uncertain path. Professor Boykin fears that as
the number of nuclear weapons is reduced, verification
could become more difficult, and non-nuclear countries
could catch up more quickly with the superpowers, who
might then be tempted to shift to the production of
biological and chemical weapons of warfare. In urging
the United States and the USSR to listen to the voices
of other countries and peoples alarmed by the nuclear
arms race between the superpowers, Ambassador Jack
Perry asks whether the Chinese might oppose any
superpower agreement which would enable the USSR to
point its missiles away from the United States and
toward China. Further, as long as the USSR relies upon
nuclear power to control its Eastern European empire,
he suggests that the collective voice of these nations
will have little chance of reducing the size of the
Soviet nuclear arsenal. Similarly, as Professor Edward
Davis asserts, as long as NATO's conventional forces
and strategic doctrines continue to lag behind those of
the Warsaw Pact, the United States must rely on nuclear
weapons to protect, if not control, its European
allies. Both Perry and Davis conclude, however, that
limiting and eliminating nuclear weapons depends upon
symmetry and balance of forces. For Davis, a balance
between the Warsaw Pact and NATO of conventional forces
will make nuclear force reductions possible. For
Perry, the weight of additional voices vitally
concerned about the ominous sounds of the nuclear
dialogue will counterbalance the myopic concern of the
superpowers with their own interests, and compel them
to weigh carefully their responsibilities to other
voices in the worldwide nuclear dilemma.

Ambassador Kenneth Adelman maintains that the
United States and the USSR have indeed achieved a
strategic balance resting on nuclear weapons. Although
he credits this balance with preserving for some 40
years a general peace, he strongly believes that the
time has come to move away from dependence upon nuclear
weapons to maintain this peace--a policy bearing the
depressing acronym MAD, for Mutual Assured Destruction.
Adelman sees the Reagan Administration's Strategic
Defense Initiative (SDI) as the defensive alternative
to the offensive-minded nuclear deterrence of MAD.
Asserting the case for a defensive strategic
equilibrium, he says that the United States is behind
the USSR in research on defensive methods and systems
of deterrence and needs SDI to keep us even with Soviet
progress.

This assertion differs from Ambassador Raymond
Garthoff's view that the USSR lags behind the United
States in strategic defensive weapons research.
History shows, according to Garthoff, however, that the
Soviets have never been very far behind us in strategic
weapons research, and any leads we have gained have not

lasted very long. Yet, contends Garthoff, even when
the USSR duplicates SDI, it will increase and keep open
its options for offensive systems, thereby endangering
anew the symmetry and balance of strategic forces.
Instead of increasing security and stabilizing
superpower relations, SDI will, maintains Garthoff,
have precisely the opposite effects.

In an approach similar to Ambassador Garthoff's
analysis of the historical development of the USSR's
nuclear weapons policy, Professor Jamie Moore analyzes
the origins of SDI. He shows that the strategy behind
SDI has deep roots in American military history.
Traditionally, military planners have relied upon
strong defensive systems to protect the country's
security and interests. That these systems proved
irrelevant to the crises which developed did not
discourage successive strategies, including, according
to Moore, the planners and supporters of SDI. They see
the public rallying around a strategy which is rooted
in American history and are optimistic, he says, that
Congress will fund adequately the entire program.

Writing as concerned and informed members of this
public, however, Molly Ravenel and Steve Hoffius
sharply criticize SDI. They point out, as does
Garthoff, that it might touch off an arms race while at
the same time threatening to give the United States a
first strike capability. Ravenel sees SDI as a threat
to the continuation of the ABM Treaty and Hoffius
contends that it does nothing to reduce and eliminate
existing stockpiles of nuclear weapons.

Several contributors to this study expressed grave
concerns indeed about the implications of these vast
stockpiles of nuclear weapons and the consequences of
their spread to other nations, less advanced and
prosperous. Professor Mark Garrison believes that a
fundamental characteristic of Americans toward others
is embodied in a "live-and-let-live" approach. This
concept is roughly congruent with putting the highest
priority on avoiding nuclear war. He sees SDI as a
positive indication of the Reagan Administration's
commitment ot this priority, linking SDI, as does
Pofessor Moore, to an important American tradition.
The proof of this commitment to avoid nuclear war,
Garrison asserts, is to dedicate our energies to
reducing our own store of nuclear weapons, while
increasing the strength of our conventional forces to
guard our fundamental interests.

Professors Dagobert Brito and Michael Intriligator
see additional dangers in the number of nuclear weapons
as well as their proliferation among less advanced and
prosperous nations. The all-destructive danger of
these weapons has already allowed minor powers like
Cuba to exploit the rivalry of the superpowers to
obtain economic and political concessions while
bringing them to the edge of war. Further exploitation
could lead to more danger and instability and a
continuing unfair distribution of wealth and power.

Brito and Intriligator contend that the elimination of
their nuclear weapons would enable the superpowers to
prevent this kind of exploitation. Rather than nuclear
weapons, they should develop and rely upon conventionally armed ballistic missiles of such power and
accuracy that no lesser nation could afford the risk
and cost of possessing and securing a nuclear arsenal.

Implicit in a number of the essays in this volume
and explicit in those of Adelman, Boykin, and Garrison
is concern about the morality of the possession as well
as the use of nuclear weapons. Adelman asserts that
maintaining peace through the defensive-minded system
of SDI rather than through offensive-minded nuclear
deterrence is more moral and ethical. Boykin contends
that a moral commitment to preserve civilization from
nuclear holocaust should be the guiding principle for
negotiations between the superpowers. Finally,
Garrison asks whether any of our national goals could
be as important as that of avoiding nuclear war.

As this is written, prospects for some agreement
on nuclear weapons between the U. S. and the USSR seem
more promising than during our Symposium in early 1985.
In Geneva, arms control talks have resumed, and at a
two-day meeting in Reykjavik, Iceland, on 11-12 October
1986, President Reagan and General Secretary Gorbachev
rather suddenly met in what the President termed a
"pre-summit." Their negotiations raised a number of
key issues--the Reagan Administratin's commitment to
SDI and the Soviet linkage of it to future arms control
agreements; the rather unsettling idea of eliminating
all strategic ballistic missiles in ten years; and the
proposed eradication of intermediate missiles in Europe
and the reduction to 100 SS-20 warheads in Asia.
During the negotiations, the two sides seemed to have
moved closer to an accommodation on these issues, but
in the end, they were unable to reconcile their
fundamental differences over SDI.

The failure of the Reykjavik Summit seemed to have
derailed the summit process and dramatized the
fragility of the U. S. - Soviet relationship. And the
Reagan Administration's absorption with the Iran-Contra
affair appeared to have diverted its attention almost
completely from arms control issues. Then, almost as
suddenly as he proposed the meeting which took place in
Reykjavik, Secretary Gorbachev announced that the
Soviet delegation would put forth at Geneva new
proposals to eliminate intermediate range nuclear
missiles in Europe and reduce SS-20 warheads in Asia to
100. Neither proposal, he stated, would be linked to
discussions on SDI. Anxious to rise above the Iran-
Contra imbroglio and apparently eager to restore hope
and a sense of fulfillment to the arms control process,
the Administration responded very positively to the
Soviet proposals and advanced significant corrolaries
of its own. Certainly major differences in policies on
arms control and nuclear weapons remain, but just as
clear is the opportunity now for major agreements. It

is our hope that the concepts and plans which arose at
The Citadel Symposium on Arms Control and Nuclear
Weapons will bring forth fresh insight and
encouragement to those who must resolve the conundrum
of arms control and nuclear weapons.

Bibliography

Adelman, Kenneth L. "Summitry: The Historical
    Perspective." Presidential Quarterly: Leadership
    and National Security Policy 16, no. 3 (Summer
    1986): 435-41.

Allan, Pierre. Crisis Bargaining and the Arms Race: A
    Theoretical Model. Cambridge, Mass.: Ballinger
    Publishing Co., 1983.

Arkin, William M., and Richard W. Fieldhouse. Nuclear
    Battlefields: Global Links in the Arms Race.
    Cambridge, Mass.: Ballinger Publishing Co., 1985.

Aviation Week and Space Technology, April 21, 1986.

Bark, Dennis L., ed. To Promote Peace: U.S. Foreign
    Policy in the Mid-1980s. Stanford, Calif.:
    Hoover Institution Press, 1984.

Baugh, William H. The Politics of Nuclear Balance:
    Ambiguity and Continuity in Strategic Policies.
    New York: Longman, 1984.

Beres, Louis R. Reason and Realpolitik: U.S. Foreign
    Policy and World Order. Lexington, Mass.: D. C.
    Heath, 1984.

Berman, Robert P., and John C. Baker. Soviet Strategic
    Forces: Requirements and Responses. Washington,
    D.C.: Brookings Institution, 1982.

Blechman, Barry M., ed. Rethinking the U.S. Strategic
    Posture. Cambridge, Mass.: Ballinger Publishing,
    1982.

Bornstein, Morris, Zvi Gitelman, and William Zimmerman,
    eds. East-West Relations and the Future of
    Eastern Europe. London: George Allen & Unwin,
    1982.

Boutwell, Jeffrey D., Paul Doty, and Gregory F.
    Treverton, eds. The Nuclear Confrontation in
    Europe. Dover, Mass.: Auburn House Publishing
    Co., 1985.

Bracken, Paul. The Command and Control of Nuclear
    Forces. New Haven, Conn.: Yale University Press,
    1983.

Brauch, Hans G. Decisionmaking for Arms Limitation:
    Assessments and Prospects. Cambridge, Mass.:
    Ballinger Publishing Co., 1983.

Brito, D. L., A. M. Buoncristiani, and M. D.
    Intriligator. "A New Approach to the Nash
    Bargaining Problem" Econometrica 45 (1977):
    1163-72

_____. "Proliferation and the Probability
    of War: Global and Regional Issues" in D. L.
    Brito, M. D. Intriligator, and A. E. Wick, eds.
    Strategies for Managing Nuclear
    Proliferation--Economic and Political Issues,
    Lexington, Mass.: Lexington Books, 1983.

Broadhurst, Arlene Idol, ed. The Future of European
    Alliance Systems: NATO and the Warsaw Pact.
    Boulder, Colo.: Westview Press, 1982.

Brodie, Bernard. War and Politics. New York:
    Macmillan Publishing Co., Inc., 1973.

_____. Strategy in the Missile Age.
    Princeton: Princeton University Press, 1959.

Brodie, Bernard, et al. National Security and
    International Stability. Cambridge, Mass.:
    Oelgeschlager, Gunn & Hain, Publishers, 1983.

_____. The Absolute Weapon: Atomic Power
    and World Order. New York: 1946.

Brown, Harold. Thinking about National Security:
    Defense and Foreign Policy in a Dangerous World.
    Boulder, Colo.: Westview Press, 1983.

Bueno de Mesquita, B. The War Trap New Haven: Yale
    University Press, 1971.

Burrows, Bernard, and Geoffrey Edwards. The Defense
    of Western Europe. London: Butterworth
    Scientific, 1982.

Caldwell, Dan, ed. Soviet International Behavior and
    U.S. Policy Options. Lexington, Mass.: Lexington
    Books, 1983.

Cimbala, Stephen, ed. National Security Strategy:
    Choices and Limits. New York: Praeger
    Publishers, 1984.

Coffey, Joseph I. Arms Control and European Security.
    New York: Praeger Publishers for the
    International Institute for Strategic Studies,
    1977.

Collins, John M. U.S. Military Balance, 1980-1985.
    New York: Pergamon-Brassey's, 1985.

Cox, Arthur Macy. Russian Roulette: The Superpower
    Game. New York: Times Books, 1982.

Dahlitz, Julie. Nuclear Arms Control with Effective
    International Agreements. London and Boston:
    George Allen & Unwin, 1983.

Dunn, Keith A., and William O. Staudenmaier.
    Alternative Military Strategies for the Future.
    Boulder, Colo.: Westview Press, 1985.

Ellison, Herbert J., ed. Soviet Policy toward Western
    Europe: Implications for the Atlantic Alliance.
    Seattle: University of Washington Press, 1984.

Fedder, Edwin H., ed. Defense Politics of the
    Atlantic Alliance. New York: Praeger Publishers,
    1980.

Feis, Herbert. Japan Subdued: The Atomic Bomb and
    the End of the War in the Pacific. Princeton:
    Princeton University Press, 1961.

Feld, Werner J., and John K. Wildgren. NATO and the
    Atlantic Defense: Perceptions and Illusions. New
    York: Praeger Publishers, 1982.

Flynn, Gregory, and Hans Rattinger, eds. The Public
    and Atlantic Defense. Totowa, N.J.: Rowman &
    Allanheld, Publishers, 1985.

Frei, Daniel. Assumptions and Perceptions in
    Disarmament. New York: United Nations
    Publications, 1984.

Frei, Daniel, and Christian Catrina. Risks of
    Unintentional Nuclear War. Totowa, N.J.:
    Allanheld, Osmun, 1983.

Gabriel, R. A. Military Incompetence. New York: Hill &
    Wang, 1985.

Galtung, Johan. Environment, Development, and Military
    Activity: Towards Alternative Security Doctrines.
    Oslo: Universitatsforlaget, 1982.

Garthoff, Raymond L. Perspectives on the Strategic
     Balance. Washington, D.C.: Brookings
     Institution, 1983.

_____. Detente and Confrontation: American
     Soviet Relations from Nixon to Reagan.
     Washington, D.C.: Brookings Institution, 1985.

Gayler, Noel. "A Commander-in-Chief's Perspective." In
     The Nuclear Crisis Reader. Vintage Books, 1984.

Giovannitti, L., and F. Freed. The Decision to Drop
     the Bomb. New York: Coward-McCann, Inc., 1965.

Golden, James R., et al. Conventional Deterrence:
     Alternatives for European Defense. Lexington,
     Mass.: D. C. Heath, 1984.

Green, William C. Soviet Nuclear Weapons Policy:
     Research Guide. Boulder, Colo.: Westview Press,
     1986.

Hagen, Lawrence S. ed. The Crisis in Western
     Security. New York: St. Martin's Press, 1982.

Haley, P. Edward, David M. Keithly, and Jack Merritt.
     Nuclear Strategy, Arms Control, and the Future.
     Boulder, Colo.: Westview Press, 1985.

Harries-Jenkins, Gwyn, ed. Armed Forces and the
     Welfare Societies: Challenges in the 1980s:
     Britain, the Netherlands, Germany, Sweden, and the
     United States. New York: St. Martin's Press,
     1983.

Herken, Gregg. The Winning Weapon: The Atomic Bomb
     in the Cold War, 1945-50. New York: Alfred A.
     Knopf, 1980.

_____. Counsels of War. New York: Alfred
     A. Knopf, 1985.

Holloway, David. The Soviet Union and the Arms Race.
     New Haven, Conn.: Yale University Press, 1983.

Holloway, David, and Jane M. O. Sharp, eds. The Warsaw
     Pact: Alliance in Transition? Ithaca, N. Y.:
     Cornell University Press, 1984.

Holm, Hans-Henrik, and Nikolaj Petersen, eds. The
     European Missiles Crisis: Nuclear Weapons and
     Security Policy. New York: St. Martin's Press,
     1983.

Houston Post, April 28, 1986.

Hunter, Robert E. NATO, The Next Generation. Boulder,
    Colo.: Westview Press, 1984.

Jackson, Robert J., ed. Continuity of Discord: Crises
    and Responses in the Atlantic Community. New
    York: Praeger Publishers, 1985.

Jane's Fighting Ships 1984-85 London: Jane's
    Publishing Company, Limited.

Jervis, Robert. The Illogic of American Nuclear
    Strategy. Ithaca, N.Y.: Cornell University
    Press, 1984.

Johnson, James Turner. Can Modern War Be Just? New
    Haven, Conn.: Yale University Press, 1984.

Kaplan, Fred. The Wizards of Armageddon: Strategists
    of the Nuclear Age. New York: Simon & Schuster,
    1983.

Kennan, George. "The Sources of Soviet Conduct."
    Foreign Affairs 25 (July 1947): 556-82.

_____. The Nuclear Delusion: Soviet-American
    Relations in the Atomic Age. New York: Pantheon
    Books, 1976, 1983.

Kennedy, Robert. The Defense of the West: Strategic
    and European Security Issues Reappraised.
    Boulder, Colo.: Westview Press, 1984.

Kissinger, Henry A. Nuclear Weapons and Foreign
    Policy. New York: W. W. Norton & Co., Inc.,
    1957, 1969.

Kroes, Rob. "Cruise Missiles": Armed Forces and
    Society 12, no. 4 (Summer 1986): pp. 581-90.

Laird, Robbin R., and Dale R. Herspring. The Soviet
    Union and Strategic Arms. Boulder, Colo.:
    Westview Press, 1984.

Liddell-Hart, B. H. History of the Second World War.
    New York: G. P. Putnam's Sons, 1970.

Litwak, Robert S. Detente and the Nixon Doctrine:
    American Foreign Policy and the Pursuit of
    Stability, 1969-1976. New York: Cambridge
    University Press, 1984.

Lockwood, Jonathan S. The Soviet View of U.S.
    Strategic Doctrine: Implications for Decision
    Making. New Brunswick, N.J.: Transaction Books,
    1983.

Luck, Edward C., ed. Arms Control: The Multilateral
    Alternative. New York: New York University
    Press, 1983.

Maghroori, Ray, and Bennett Ramberg. Globalism versus
    Realism: International Relations' Third Debate.
    Boulder, Colo.: Westview Press, 1982.

Malone, Peter. The British Nuclear Deterrent. London:
    Croom Helm Ltd., 1984.

Markey, Edward J. Nuclear Peril, The Politics of
    Proliferation. Cambridge, Mass.: Ballinger,
    1982.

Mearsheimer, John J. Conventional Deterrence. Ithaca,
    N.Y.: Cornell University Press, 1983.

_____. "Nuclear Weapons and Deterrence
    in Europe." International Security 9 (Winter
    1984/85): 19-46.

Melanson, Richard A. Neither Nuclear Cold War nor
    Detente? Soviet-American Relations in the 1980's.
    Charlottesville: University Press of Virginia,
    1982.

Meyer, Stephen M. The Dynamics of Nuclear
    Proliferation. Chicago: University of Chicago
    Press, 1984.

Mitchell, R. Judson. Ideology of a Superpower:
    Contemporary Soviet Doctrine on International
    Relations. Stanford, Calif.: Hoover Institution
    Press, 1982.

Moreton, Edwina, and Gerald Segal, eds. Soviet
    Strategy toward Western Europe. Winchester,
    Mass.: Allen & Unwin, 1984.

Mosley, Hugh G. The Arms Race: Economic and Social
    Consequences. Lexington, Mass.: Lexington Books,
    1985.

Musa, Mark and Peter Bondanella, eds. The Portable
    Machiavelli. Penguin Books, 1979.

Myers, Kenneth A. ed. NATO: The Next Thirty Years.
    Boulder, Colo.: Westview Press, 1980.

Nacht, Michael. The Age of Vulnerability: Threats to
    the Nuclear Stalemate. Washington, D.C.: The
    Brookings Institution, 1985.

Nash, J. F. "The Bargaining Problem." Econometrica
    18 (1956): 155-62.

National Conference of Catholic Bishops. The Challenge
    of Peace: God's Promise and Our Response: A
    Pastoral Letter on War and Peace. May 3, 1983.

Newhouse, John. Cold Dawn: The Story of SALT. New
    York: Holt, Rinehart & Winston, 1973.

New York Times, April 26, 1986.

North Atlantic Treaty Organization: Facts and
    Figures. Brussels: NATO Information Service,
    1981.

Nurick, Robert, ed. Nuclear Weapons and European
    Security. New York: St. Martin's Press, 1984.

Nye, Joseph S., Jr., ed. The Making of America's
    Soviet Policy. New Haven, Conn.: Yale University
    Press, 1984.

Pfaltzgraff, Robert L., Jr., ed. Contrasting
    Approaches to Strategic Arms Control. Lexington,
    Mass.: Lexington Books, 1974.

Pipes, Daniel. "Fundamentalist Muslims Between America
    and Russia." Foreign Affairs (Summer 1986)
    939-59.

Potter, William C. Verification and Arms Control.
    Lexington, Mass.: Lexington Books, 1985.

Prados, John. The Soviet Estimate: U.S. Intelligence
    Analysis and Russian Military Strength. New York:
    The Dial Press, 1982.

Ramsey, Paul. The Just War: Force and Political
    Responsibility. New York: University Press of
    America, 1983.

Reagan, Ronald. Speech, March 23, 1983. Interview
    with the New York Times, February 12, 1985.

Reagan, Ronald. "The Strategic Defense Initiative"
    Department of State, Special Report No. 129, June
    1985.

Russett, Bruce M. Arms Control and the Arms Race:
    Readings from Scientific American. New York: W.
    H. Freeman, 1985.

Schelling, T. C. "Comments" In D. L. Brito, M. D.
    Intriligator and A. E. Wick, eds. Strategies for
    Managing Nuclear Proliferation--Economic and
    Political Issues. Lexington, Mass.: Lexington
    Books, 1983.

Schwartz, David N. NATO's Nuclear Dilemmas.
    Washington, D.C.: The Brookings Institution, 1983.

Scowcroft, Brent, Lt. Gen. Testimony before the
    Committee on Foreign Relations. In President's
    Commission on Strategic Forces. (Wednesday, May
    11, 1983.)

Scowcroft, Brent, et al. Second Report of the
    President's Commission on Strategic Forces.
    Washingnton, D. C.: Government Printing Office,
    1984.

Segal, Gerald, et al. Nuclear War and Nuclear Peace.
    New York: St. Martin's Press, 1983.

Sigal, Leon V. Nuclear Forces in Europe: Enduring
    Dilemmas, Present Prospects. Washington, D.C.:
    The Brookings Institution, 1984.

Smith, Gerard. Doubletalk: The Story of the First
    Strategic Arms Limitations Talks. Garden City,
    N.Y.: Doubleday & Company, Inc., 1980.

Sonnenfeldt, Helmut. Soviet Style in International
    Politics. The Washington Institute for Values in
    Public Policy, 1985.

Speer, A. Inside the Third Reich New York: Macmillan
    Publishing Co., Inc., 1970.

Talbott, Strobe. Endgame: The Inside Story of SALT
    II. New York: Harper & Row, Publishers, 1979.

_____. Deadly Gambits: The Reagan
    Administration and the Stalemate in Nuclear Arms
    Control. New York: Alfred A. Knopf, 1984.

Taylor, William J. Strategic Responses to Conflict in
    the 1980's. Lexington, Mass.: Lexington Books,
    1984.

Terry, Sarah M., ed. Soviet Policy in Eastern Europe.
    New Haven, Conn.: Yale University Press, 1984.

Thompson, Kenneth W. Words and Deeds in Foreign Policy.
    Fifth Morgenthau Memorial Lecture on Morality and
    Foreign Policy. Council on Foreign Affairs, 1986.

Thompson, Starley, and Stephen H. Schneider. "Nuclear
    Winter Reappraised." Foreign Affairs (Summer
    1986): 981-1005.

Thorton, Richard C. Soviet Asian Strategy in the
    Brezhnev Era and Beyond. The Washington Institute
    for Values in Public Policy, 1985.

Thucydides. History of the Peloponnesian War. Trans.
    Rex Warner N. Y.: Penguin Books, 1956, 1977.

Treverton, Gregory F. Making the Alliance Work: The
    United States and Western Europe. Ithaca, N.Y.:
    Cornell University Press, 1985.

Turco, Richard, O. Brian Toon, Thomas Ackerman, James
    Pollack, and Carl Sagan. "Nuclear Winter: Global
    Consequences of Multiple Nuclear Explosions,"
    Science, Dec. 23, 1987, 1283-92.

Turner, John. The Arms Race. Cambridge and New York:
    Cambridge University Press, 1983.

Tyroler, Charles, III. Alerting America: The Papers
    of the Committee on the Present Danger. New York:
    Pergamon Brassey's, 1984.

United States Arms Control and Disarmament Agency.
    Arms Control and Disarmament Agreements: Texts
    and Histories of Negotiations. Washington, D.C.,
    1982.

United States Department of Defense. Soviet Military
    Power, 4th ed. Washington, D.C.: U.S. Government
    Printing Office, 1986.

Vigeveno, Guido. The Bomb and European Security.
    Bloomington: Indiana University Press, 1983.

Voter Options on Nuclear Arms Policy. New York: The
    Public Agenda Foundation, 1984, pp. 50-69.

Weigley, Russell F. The American Way of War: A
    History of United States Military Strategy and
    Policy. New York and London: Macmillan, 1973.

Wildavsky, Aaron ed. Beyond Containment: Alternative
    American Policies toward the Soviet Union. San
    Francisco: Institute for Contemporary Studies,
    1983.

Wolfe, Thomas W. The SALT Experience. Cambridge,
    Mass.: Ballinger Publishing Co., 1979.

Wyden, Peter. Day One: Before Hiroshima and After.
    New York: Simon & Schuster, 1984.

Index

About the Contributors

KENNETH L. ADELMAN is Director, U.S. Arms Control and Disarmament Agency. Previously he served as Deputy Permanent Representative of the U.S. to the United Nations, and led the U.S. delegation to the U.N. Second Special Session on Disarmament. The author of numerous articles in Foreign Affairs, Foreign Policy, Harper's, The New York Times, The Wall Street Journal and The Washington Post, Mr. Adelman received his doctorate in political theory from Georgetown University.

LARRY H. ADDINGTON is Professor of Military History, The Citadel, The Military College of South Carolina. He received his doctorate in history from Duke University where he specialized in modern military history. He has lectured at the Army War College, the Naval War College, and the Army Command and General Staff College. He is the author of The Blitzkrieg Era and the German General Staff, 1865-1941 and Patterns of War since the Eighteenth Century. He is also the author of articles on nuclear arms control.

MILTON L. BOYKIN is Professor and Head of the Department of Political Science, The Citadel, Military College of South Carolina. Most recently he is coeditor of Citizens-Sailors in a Changing Society: Policy Issues for Manning the United States Naval Reserve. He has also done research for The National Defense University concerned with the Reserve Forces of NATO.

DAGOBERT L. BRITO is Peterkin Professor of Political Economy at Rice University, and MICHAEL D. INTRILIGATOR is Professor of Economics and Political Science at the University of California, Los Angeles and Director of the UCLA Center for International and Strategic Affairs.

EDWARD B. DAVIS is Associate Professor of Political Science at The Citadel, Military College of South Carolina. He received his AB from VMI, MA and Ph.D. from the University of Virginia. His primary research interest is National Security Policy.

RAYMOND L. GARTHOFF is a Senior Fellow at the Brookings Institute and served as Ambassador to Bulgaria from 1977 to 1979. He began his diplomatic career at the Department of State in 1961, and has been a member of a number of U.S. delegations dealing with arms control and nuclear weapons. From 1969 to 1972 he was Senior Advisor to the US-USSR Strategic Arms Limitation Talks in Helsinki, Vienna and Geneva. A guest lecturer at numerous universities and governmental seminars, he is a graduate of Princeton and Yale Universities.

MARK GARRISON is Director of the Center for Foreign Policy Development and Fellow of the Council for International Studies at Brown University. A member of the Council on Foreign Relations in New York, he has held posts in U.S. embassies in Hong Kong, Bulgaria, and Czechoslovakia and served as Deputy Ambassador in the embassy in Moscow. He also has held posts in the Department of State, including that of Director, Office of Soviet Union Affairs. His writings include studies and position papers for the President, National Security Council, and Secretary of State dealing with Soviet policy.

STEPHEN HOFFIUS is a journalist living in Charleston, S.C. He has worked as staffperson or consultant for a number of South Carolina citizens' organizations, including the South Carolina Nuclear Weapons Freeze Campaign.

JAMIE W. MOORE is Professor of History at The Citadel, Military College of South Carolina and a member of the Historical Advisory Committee of the Department of the Army. He received his AB from Denison University, his MA from the Univeristy of Arkansas, and his Ph.D. from the University of North Carolina. His primary interest is in American Diplomatic History. His publications include monographs and articles on the Corps of Engineers, 19th century defense concepts, and 20th century diplomacy.

W. GARY NICHOLS is Professor of History, The Citadel, Military College of South Carolina. He received his AB, MA, and Ph.D. from the University of Alabama. He has delivered a number of papers and

written articles on European diplomatic and American
Military history.

JACK R. PERRY is a retired Foreign Service Officer
whose last post abroad was as Ambassador to Bulgaria
from 1979 to 1981. From 1982 to 1985 he was John C.
West Professor of Government and International Studies
at The Citadel, Military College of South Carolina. He
is now director of the Dean Rusk Program in
International Studies and Professor of Political
Science at Davidson College.

MOLLY RAVENEL is currently the President of the Board
of Charleston YWCA. She received her AB from Smith
College in 1953 and her MA (History) from Hunter
College in 1967. She served on the National Governing
Board of Common Cause from 1975-1985. She was also the
former President of the Charleston Democratic Women.

GEORGE M. SEIGNIOUS, II, U.S.A. Ret., is currently
Chairman of the Atlantic Council of the United States,
a national and bipartisan center for the formulation of
policy recommendations on the problems and
opportunities shared by the democracies of Western
Europe, North America, Japan, Australia and New
Zealand. He graduated from The Citadel in 1942, and,
following a military career spanning more than three
decades, returned to his alma mater as president in
1974. In September 1977, President Carter appointed
him Delegate-at-Large on the U.S. delegation to the
SALT negotiations at Geneva. In 1979, March to
mid-December he served as Director of the U.S. Arms
Control and Disarmament Agency.

65981